Project Success Factors In Digital Age

Research Results

Burak Uluocak, Ph.D.

DEDICATION

To my family who made me a better person: Tamara, Şener, Buket, my dear wife Neslihan and my daughter Yağmur.

CONTENTS

ACKNOWLEDGMENTS

There have been many people who supported, helped and provided guidance during the preparation of this book.

I would like to express my gratitude to my dissertation advisor Prof. Dr. Atilla Dicle, who has supported me since my MBA studies. His comments, contributions and guidance helped me not only to achieve a higher standard in my Ph.D. process, but also led me to mature personally and professionally as well.

I would also like to thank Prof. Dr. Ali Erkan Eke and Prof. Dr. Beril Durmuş for their contributions and support not only during my thesis, but also during their lectures that affected me deeply. I would also like to thank Prof. Dr. Güner Gürsoy for his guidance and contributions.

1 INTRODUCTION

IT projects are considered as more complex and less predictable than other types of projects such as engineering and construction (Ewusi-Mensah, 1997). These projects often exceed their proposed budgets and/or schedules and do not always fulfill their objectives.

In the last decades, some publications have addressed the issue of IT projects being behind schedule, over budgeted and not meeting stakeholder anticipations (Mahaney & Lederer, 2006; Hartman & Ashrafi, 2002). According to Project Management Institute's (PMI) 2012 Pulse Report, only half of the projects meet their original schedule and budget targets and contribute to the organization's strategic goals. These projects are considered as failure (or unsuccessful).

Today, the ability of a company to use its technology know-how usually brings a competitive advantage and it is an important topic in general strategy. The companies and IT departments that provide technology services to sectors as telecommunications, banking, retail and logistics are in a serious competition. Companies try to present new products in the shortest available time with the best quality in order to compete in their markets. As a result, the importance given to the management of product development projects is rapidly growing. Most of the information technology companies or departments have project management offices (PMOs) and the number of Project Management Institute certified professionals are growing in a continuous way.

The major aim of this book is to analyze project success criteria in order to identify the project success understanding, and to identify the project management success factors and their influence on project performance in IT sector.

The secondary purpose of the study is to determine the moderating effects of project duration and organization structure on project management success factors and project performance relationship in IT sector.
Studies about project management are very popular; on the other hand, there is no general agreement or standard on project success definitions or how to measure it (Culler, 2009). A project which is considered as a successful project by a team member may be considered as an unsuccessful project for another team member. Lim & Mohammed (1999) points out "all the stakeholders in a project can hardly hold the same point of view on this matter."

Baker, Murphy, and Fisher (1974) concludes "there is probably no such thing as a complete success in project management; there is only perceived success of the project."

Addition to these, success evaluation changes over time. For example, a project which is deployed on time and budget may be considered as a very successful project at first. Besides, if quality problems are discovered later or product does not reach to target market shares, the same project will be viewed as an unsuccessful one.

In the literature, there are no consistent research results related to relationships between project success factors and IT project performance (Culler, 2009; Westlund, 2007; Agirre Perez, 2007; Wu, 2006Hass, 2006; Nasr, 2004).

On the other hand, it is quite important for project practitioners to understand the degree of relationships between critical success factors and information technology project performance in order to concentrate on the right factor at the right time to reach the desired project success.

2 HISTORY OF PROJECT MANAGEMENT

The history of project management begins with large-scale construction objectives. To complete the constructions, different groups had to work together toward a common goal by organizing tasks while maintaining relationships between tasks. Evidence of project management methodology was found in Egyptian architectural artifacts (Frame, 2003; Richman, 2002). The Egyptians exhibited project management behaviors during the Egyptian pyramid constructions, which required coordinating tasks and people with different skill sets. Shenhar and Dvir (2007) state that The Roman Aqueducts, Hadrian's Wall, the Great Wall of China, and the Taj Mahal are also some examples of great projects and project management applications from the history. On the other hand, project management did not evolve into a recognized discipline until the 20th century.

Murch (2001) points out that the scientific management - introduced by Frederick Taylor – which includes examining each job to define optimum procedures, matching tasks with necessary skills, recording worker performance and management of all work, is the basis of modern project management.

Many project management techniques started to be used in the United States military projects during World War I. The Gantt chart developed by Henry Gantt for representing the schedules graphically for the construction of U.S. Navy ships was one of these techniques (Murch, 2001). Gantt chart technique is still widely used for planning, monitoring and performance measurement purposes in modern project management.

On the other hand, line managers were functioning as project managers during the 1940s. According to Kerzner (2010) each line manager was performing the work necessary for his / her line organization and giving the responsibility to another line manager when his / her part was finished. The problem with this type of management was that the clients and customers had no single contact point when needed.

During the Cold War, mass destruction weapons started to be produced in the United States. Development of these weapons involved potentially thousands of contractors. Kerzner indicates that at this point the government needed a single point of contact, project manager, who had total accountability through all project phases.

As a result in 1950s and 1960s, project management techniques were formalized with methods and tools created to manage aerospace projects. The U.S. Department of Defense (DOD) and the National Aeronautics and Space Administration (NASA) set standards for contractors concerning project management practices (Kerzner, 2010). According to Marchewka (2006), The Program Evaluation Review Technique (PERT) was one of these methods to examine and determine the involved tasks and their durations in order to identify the minimum time needed to finish the total project. The Critical Path Method (CPM) was another useful method first used during the development of the U.S. Navy Polaris submarine, in order to calculate the longest path of planned activities, and the earliest / latest time each activity can start and finish without lengthening the project.

On the other hand, Kerzner points out that private industry viewed these practices as an unnecessary management cost and saw no practical value in project management. According to him, in the 1960s, excluding defense, aerospace, and construction sectors, the majority of companies and sectors maintained informal methods for the management of their projects. In informal project management, the authority of the project manager was minimized. Projects were handled by functional managers and formal communications were handled informally related to the good relationships between line managers.

Since, the size and complexity of the projects had grown to serious levels, more companies departed from informal ways and started to formalize project management processes, in the 1970s and 1980s (Kerzner, 2010). According to Alfi (2002) the early 1980s marked the beginning of modern project-based organizations. Project management researchers published data, developed theories, and established industry-accepted practices.

Kerzner points out that during the 1980s, a paradigm shift related to project success factors occurred within the project management field from the quantitative factors to qualitative factors. The literature began to include information on qualitative factors such as low morale and the lack of motivation. Other qualitative factors receiving attention pertained to human relations deficiency with low productivity and employees lacking commitment or functional obligation. Researchers during the 1980s also began studying problems related to solving delays and the delay in resolving policy issues along with conflicting priorities among stakeholders.

By the 1990s, companies and organizations realized that implementing formal project management was not a choice, but a necessity. As a result, by 2000s, project management has spread to virtually every industry (Kerzner, 2010). According to Alfi economic, social, and technological driving forces have caused a continued corporate change from highly centralized, hierarchical, and top down structures towards decentralized project based organizational structures.

Glen (2005) reports that, in the past, clients in the IT sector frequently challenged the requirement for a project manager with the reasoning that a programmer was doing all the work. Today a concern regarding the requirement for a project manager rarely arises anymore, because organization leaders accept project management as the best practice. In their research on project performance, Ashrafi and Hartman (2002), points out that if project management improves, cost and time can be reduced by more than 25% while profits will increase by 5% in high tech companies.

According to Heerkens (2002), the main objective of a project is to achieve a business result such as increasing sales, making operations more efficient or improving effectiveness. The final purpose of every project is simple: to save money or to make money.
Today, projects turn corporate strategies into reality (Crawford and Pennypacker 2002). They are the vehicles for strategic plan deployment in companies because strategic plans are composed of projects that are designed to deliver a company's strategic plan. For example, strategic projects must reach successful completion to achieve profitability forecasts associated with predefined business opportunities. If projects are failing (from a strategic plan perspective), then, this means companies are not making the projected profits.

Related to Project Management Institute's Annual Report (2013), the value of project management is highly recognized in every corner of the world:

- The Indian government's 12th Five-Year Plan mentions project management as a capability that should be learned and standardized in order to improve efficiency.

- The U.S. Government Efficiency Caucus was established in 2012, in order to make the U.S. government more efficient by increasing the usage of program management.

- Major Projects Leadership Academy was launched by the The UK government to develop the skills of project leaders across government for delivering complex projects.

- Finally, South Korea government issued a law for the establishment of program management offices.

3 DEFINITION OF PROJECT AND PROJECT MANAGEMENT

According to Merriam Webster Dictionary, the first known use of the word "project" is 15th century and it comes from the Latin word projectum, past principle of proicere, to throw forward. "Pro-" means something that precedes the action of the next part of the word in time and "jacere" means to throw. The word "project" thus originally meant "something that comes before anything else is done." When the word was initially adopted, it referred to a plan of something, not to the act of carrying this plan out.

Project Management Institute's Project Management Body of Knowledge (PMBOK) (2008), defines the term project as "a temporary endeavor undertaken to create a unique product, service or result."

International Project Management Association (IPMA) (2006) defines project as "time and cost constrained operation to realize a set of defined deliverables up to quality standards and requirements."

Projects in a Controlled Environment (Prince2) (2014) defines a project as "temporary organization that is created for the purpose of delivering one or more business products according to an agreed business case."

As Tuman (1983) states "A project is an organization of people dedicated to a specific purpose or objective. Projects generally involve large, expensive, unique, or high risk undertakings which have to be completed by a certain date, for a certain amount of money, within some expected level of performance. At a minimum, all projects need to have well defined objectives and sufficient resources to carry out all the required tasks."

According to the definition provided by Pinto & Slevin (1988), a project can be defined with the following characteristics:

- Specified time to completion: A defined beginning and end,
- Performance expectations: A specific goal or set of goals,
- A series of interrelated or complex activities,
- A certain budget.

Declerck et al., (1983, 1997), emphasize the political perspective of projects: "a project is a whole of actions limited in time and space, inserted in, and in interaction with a politico-socio-economic environment, aimed at and tended towards a goal progressively redefined by the dialectic between the thought (the project plan) and the reality."

In the words of Turner (1999), "a project is an endeavor in which human, financial and material resources are organized in a novel way to undertake a unique scope of work, of given specification, within constraints of cost and time, so as to achieve beneficial change defined by quantitative and qualitative objectives."

Kerzner (2006) defines a project as a temporary undertaking, designed to accomplish a specific objective, using a defined set of resources, within a specified timeframe and budget, in order to achieve defined quality goals and levels of customer satisfaction.

The temporary nature of project implies a definite beginning and an end. As the project objectives have been reached or the project is terminated, the end is reached. Temporary project does not necessarily mean short in duration. Many projects can last for years like subway projects. Also, temporary does not generally apply to the service, result or product created by the project; most projects are initiated to create a lasting deliverable.

Every project is unique. Although repetitive elements may exist in some project deliverables, the repetition does not change the uniqueness of the project work. As an example, buildings may be constructed by the same team and with the similar materials, but each location is unique.

PMBOK (2008) defines project management as "the application of knowledge, skills, tools and techniques to project activities to meet the project requirements." It is achieved by the appropriate application and integration of project management processes. These five process groups are: "Initiating, Planning, Executing, Monitoring & Controlling and Closing."

As PMBOK states project management includes:

- Identification of requirements,
- Addressing the various expectations, concerns and needs of the stakeholders,
- Supplying necessary communications among stakeholders,
- Leading the stakeholders and the team towards creating deliverables,
- Balancing the project constraints including,
  - o Resources,
  - o Schedule,
  - o Risks,
  - o Scope,
  - o Quality,
  - o Budget.

As a rule, if anyone above factor changes, at least one other is likely to be affected. For example, if the schedule is shortened, the budget may be increased in order to add new resources to complete the same work in less time. Also, the quality may be reduced, if a budget increase is not possible, in order to deliver a product in less time with the same budget. Project stakeholders may have different ideas as which factors are the most important; where changing the project requirements may trigger new risks, the project team should assess the position and balance the demands to deliver an outstanding project.

Also, the project management plan is iterative. It goes through progressive elaboration throughout the project's lifecycle. Progressive elaboration involves continuous improvement and detailed planning. As more specific information is obtained, so more accurate estimates become available.

Kerzner (2006) defines project management "as the planning, organizing, directing, and controlling of company resources for a relatively short term objective that has been established to complete specific goals and objectives." It is the application of knowledge, tools, techniques and skills to meet project requirements. It is performed by the processes such as initiating, planning, executing, controlling, and closing.

According to Seymour et al. (1992) project management is a crucial strategy for the changes that organizations are experiencing as they adapt from a stable, machine like model to a more dynamic one in the face of environmental change and turbulence. Project managers face difficult tasks of both supporting adaptability, flexibility, and the acceptance of change as a lasting state, and providing support for team members to enable them to live with the process they may experience as stressful.

An industrial project has various activities and tasks that should focus on a single goal (Lock, 2003). From the initiation of the activities to the completion and delivery of the product or service, the organization must operate on the basis of cooperation and interaction to meet the responsibilities to the client. Therefore, it is essential for an organization to have the necessary capability in planning and optimizing the project activities, management tools and methodologies in order to control cost and time constraints while meeting the challenging requirements of efficiency.

Project management is a special branch of general management which has evolved in order to control and co-ordinate the complex activities of modern industry. The changing environment of the twenty-first century business world increases the range of activities coming under the area of project management. According to Prabhakar (2008), since projects exist in an open environment, they have to respond to the changing characteristics of situations to become much more adaptive than ever.

Traditionally, the European view of project management has been wider ranging than the North American view. For European practitioners and project associations a project starts with an initiating idea and business justification and ends with the operationalization of its deliverables, often covering multiple smaller single projects. This links and overlaps project management with change management (Thiry, 2010). For example, the UK's Association of Project Management's Body of Knowledge has 52 knowledge areas, as compared with nine of the Project Management Institute's PMBOK Guide. Europeans, to some extent, describes a discipline rather than a process (IPMA, 2006; APM, 2006); in contrast, North Americans have mostly taken the view that project management is a process to manage single projects.

As PMBOK states, organizational strategies shape portfolio, program and project management. Portfolio management is related with selecting the correct programs and projects and supplying necessary resources in order to embody the strategy of the organization. Also, program management is concerned with the realization of organizational benefits by harmonizing and controlling interdependencies between program components and projects.

Etymologically, the word program derives from the Greek prographein, meaning: to write before. It has evolved in Latin and French to mean a "notice or list of a series of events" (Thiry, 2010). The PMI defines a program as "a group of related projects, subprograms, and program activities managed in a coordinated way to obtain benefits not available from managing them individually." Managing Successful Programmes (MSP) defines a program as "a temporary flexible organization created to coordinate, direct and oversee the implementation of a set of related projects and activities in order to deliver outcomes and benefits related to the organization's strategic objectives." The PMI insists on the grouping of interrelated projects for tactical reasons; MSP focuses on the organization required to deliver strategic benefits and results.

As PMBOK states programs may include other works which are outside the scope of the individual projects in the program. A program will always have projects. On the other hand, a project may or not be a part of a program. Program management is the application of techniques, tools, knowledge and skills in order to reach the program objectives and to obtain benefits and control that is cannot be reached by managing the projects individually. An example of a program can be the establishment of a communications satellite system. This program may include projects for the establishment of ground stations, design of the satellite and the construction of each, the development of the system, and the launch.

Furthermore, portfolio management is concerned with the management of sub portfolios, programs, projects and even operations in a coordinated way to realize organizational strategic objectives. As an example, a construction company may have an objective like maximization of efficiency. The company may form a portfolio that includes a mix of projects in airports, power, oil, water, gas, rail, and roads. From these areas, the company may prefer to manage related projects as a program. All the airport projects may be grouped under an airport program. Similarly, the rail projects may be grouped under a different program.

Portfolio management focuses on ensuring that programs and projects are coordinated to prioritize resource allocation and that the management of the portfolio is aligned to organization's strategies (PMBOK, 2013). Therefore, according to Thiry, portfolio management is a strictly a decision making process based on known data; it is a low –uncertainty, but high ambiguity process.

4 ORGANIZATIONAL INFLUENCES

As Robbins & Judge (2009) describes "an organization is a consciously coordinated social unit, composed of two or more people that functions on a relatively continuous basis to achieve a common goal or set of goals." According to Project Management Institute, an organization's structure, culture and style impact how projects in the organization are performed. One of the enterprise environmental factors is organizational structure of the company, which can affect influence how projects are conducted and the availability of resources. These organizational structures range from functional to projectized, with different types matrix structures.

The classical functional organization is a hierarchy where each employee has one clear superior. Staff members are grouped by their specialties, such as marketing, accounting, production and engineering. Each department will do its project work independently of others in a functional organization.

Matrix organizations show a mixture of functional and projectized characteristics. Scott (2003) states that conflicts that are observed between product and function in most of the organizations are institutionalized in matrix organizations by separating these two structure principles. While this structure does not resolve this conflict totally, it secures that both product and function interests are protected and have owners and stakeholders who will defend them in the structure. As a result, conflicts between these managers and representatives are made visible to the organization.

Matrix organizations can be classified as strong, balanced, or weak which depends on the relative level of influence and power between project and functional managers. PMI states that most of the features of a functional organization can be seen in weak matrix organizations, where the role of the project manager is more of an expediter or coordinator. A project expediter works as communication coordinator and staff assistant. He or she cannot personally make or enforce decisions. On the other hand, project coordinators have some authority, have the power to make some decisions, and may report to a higher-level manager.

Strong matrix organizations have full-time project managers with considerable authority; have many of the characteristics of the projectized organization, and full time project administrative staff. Finally, although the balanced matrix organization recognizes the need for a project manager, he or she does not have full authority on the project.

Alfi (2002) states that economic reasons for the shift towards project-based organizations are: to manage quality, maintain customer focus, continuous improvement, and reduce/control program costs. According to Kerzner (2006), in project driven organizations, all activities are characterized through projects where each project has its own profit and loss statement.

Based on PMI's definition in projectized organizations, nearly all organizational resources are involved in the project work. Project managers have superb independence and authority. The teams may report directly to the project manager and provide support to different projects.

5 PROJECT SUCCESS CRITERIA

According to Oxford Dictionary a criterion is "a standard or principle that an item is judged by". Therefore, project success criteria refer to a group of standards or principles used to judge or determine project success.

Studies about project management are quite popular; on the other hand as we have mentioned there is not a general agreement or standard on its success definitions or how to measure it (Culler, 2009). Therefore, a project which is considered as a successful project by a team member may be considered as an unsuccessful project for another team member.

For example, Baker, Murphy, and Fisher (1974) conclude that there is not any complete success in project management; there is only the perceived success of a project. They also state that success evaluation changes over time. Lim & Mohammed (1999) point out that all stakeholders of a project cannot hold the same point of view on project success. Especially in IT sector, a project which is deployed on time and budget may be considered as a very successful project at first. Besides, if quality problems are discovered later or product does not reach to target market shares, the same project will be viewed as an unsuccessful one.

Project failure and success are not necessarily contradictory or opposite notions, also they are not a "black and white" issue (Baccarni, 1999). On the other hand, most authors believe that everyone knows what is meant by "project success" or "project failure."

As Ika (2009) points out most of the authors in literature discuss general project success only as project management success. Therefore, a differentiation and separation is required between project success and project management success. Traditionally project success has been considered as the ability to fall within quality, cost and time constraints. This triple constraint, or iron triangle meets the definition of traditional project success.

On the other hand, many projects that have been delivered within cost, time, and quality have been considered as failures. At the same time, many projects that have exceeded their budget or time constraints are usually considered as successful (Pinto & Slevin, 1986).

Also as Hazebroucq (1993) suggests, projects that were identified as failures at their launch would later become models of success while others identified as successes at their launch turned into fiascos (percussion effect). A project team may, therefore, be wrongly blamed or congratulated, depending on when a project is considered as a failure or success. According to Wateridge (1998), other authors propose that quality is a subjective, multidimensional and unclear concept that lends itself to different understanding by various stakeholders.

For Munns and Bjeirmi (1996), the project management objectives are different from the project objectives. The "time / quality / cost triangle" - the most common objective of project management - should not be confused with project success.

Ika (2009) points out that the definition of project success in literature changed through time. Table 1 shows trends regarding project success and project management success. The framework involves three periods.

Research Focus	Period 1 1960s – 1980s	Period 2 1980s – 2000s	Period 3 21st Century
Success criteria	"Iron triangle" (time, quality, cost)	Iron triangle Benefits to organization Client satisfaction Benefits to project personnel Benefits to stakeholders End user's satisfaction	Iron triangle End user's satisfaction Benefits to stakeholders Benefits to project personnel Strategic objective of client organizations and business success
Success factors	Explanatory lists	Critical success factor lists and frameworks	More inclusive critical success factors frameworks and symbolic success factors
Attention	Project management success	Project / product success	Portfolio, program and project / product, success and narratives of success and failure

Table 1: Measuring Success Across Time (Ika, 2009)

The first period (between 1960s and 1980s) highlights the absolute domination of the "iron triangle" that means project management success as the criterion of project success. The second period (between 1980s and 2000s) focuses the other critical success factors as also pointed out in the work of Pinto and Slevin, "10 Critical Success Factors framework." During this time, even though the "iron triangle" was still quiet important, other success criteria were also appreciated, and the importance moved from project management success to product/ project success. For Ika (2009), the third period (21st century) welcomes strategic, portfolio and program success criteria addition to traditional project criteria.

We should not forget that, as Baccarini (1999) explains, the hard dimensions of a project like cost and time are tangible, measurable and objective. On the other hand, todays' more important criteria like stakeholder benefit and satisfaction are subjective and more difficult to measure.

Also, Jugdev & Müller (2005) mention that despite the traditional triangle view of project success is still quite important, in the last decades it is understood that broader definitions than project management success are necessary. Today, still most of the researchers, attach more importance to the cost/time/quality triangle, despite they admit that there are other criteria for success.

According to Ika (2009), project management success supports project success, but we cannot say that all successful projects are well managed. It is rational to assume that failure in project management leads to project failure, on the other hand, a project can fail despite successful project management.

Also, as Shenhar et al. (2005) put it, the target of operationally managed projects is to get the job done, on the other hand strategically managed ones are focused on business results. With this emphasis on portfolio, program and project success, it is reasonable to expect that today project success rely more on project sponsors, owners or senior managers and anyone involved in project design and selection.

According to the results of The Standish Group's final Chaos Report Survey (2014) on project success, six identified success criteria are: On-budget, on-time, on-target (requirements), on-goal (organizational strategy), valuable and satisfied. For 309 respondents, 52% chose "valuable" as the top criteria. Other results show 32% said on-budget, on-time 30%, on-target 26%, on-goal 29%, and satisfied 41%. Also, one third of the respondents selected all of the above. On the other hand, related to Standish Group's findings, if we choose all six attributes, only 1.2% of projects meet the criterion. However if we choose a single attribute, like on-budget we would be successful 42% of the time. As a result, The Standish Group advises organizations to forget the triple constraints and focus on the value of their project portfolio, not individual projects.

6 CRITICAL PROJECT SUCCESS FACTORS

Oxford Dictionary defines factor as "a fact, influence or circumstance that contributes to a result". Therefore critical project success factors indicate specifically the events, conditions and circumstances that supply project results and performance.

Previous studies in critical project success factors area were focused on the reasons for project failure instead of project success. For example, Rubin and Seeling (1967) examine the relationship between the experience of the project manager and the project's failure or success. The results of the study show that a project manager's experience had a slight impact on the project's success. Avots (1969) determines the reasons for project failure and supports that unsupportive top management, the wrong choice of the project manager and the unplanned termination of projects are the main reasons for failure. Hughes (1986) points out that projects fail as a result of the improper focus of the management, by limited communication of goals and rewarding wrong actions. However, understanding failure does not guarantee future success. According to Hawk (2006), in new projects, giving more importance to the critical success factors has been suggested as an effective method for improving project results.

Dvir et al. (1998) points out that project success factors are not common for all projects. Different projects are affected by various types of success factors. Belassi and Tukel (1996) separate these factors into four groups: project manager and team members, external environment, the project and organization. This description of critical success factors would advance improved assessment of the projects, which would as a result improve project performance.

Pinto and Slevin (1988) highlight the effect of project life cycle. In the project initiation phase, both project mission and client consultation show up as the most meaningful factors. In the planning phase, the significant factors are top management support, project mission, urgency and client acceptance. During project execution phase, the significant factors are project mission, team leader, client consultation, project schedules/plan, technical tasks and troubleshooting. Finally, at project closing phase, the most important success factors are project mission, technical tasks and client consultation.

According to Hartman and Ashrafi (2002), the current literature on software projects shows that most of the software problems are of a behavioral, management, or organizational nature, not technical.

The Standish Group (2003) collected data concerning the factors of greatest impact on IT project success. The top ten success factors are executive support, user involvement, clear business objectives, formal methodology, experienced project manager, minimized scope, agile processes, reliable estimates, standard infrastructure, and skilled staff.

Belout and Gauvreau (2004) construct a model in which the relationship between project performance and the independent variables will be affected by the project sectors, project life cycle and project structure (intervening effect).

Research in the area of success criteria and critical success factors shows that it is impossible to develop a single and complete list that will cover all types of projects. This is because the fact that success criteria and factors can differ so much from one project to another due to variables such as project scope, complexity and uniqueness (Wateridge, 1998). There is limited research on the power of the relationship between the critical factors and success criteria. Table 2 shows a summary of literature reviews on critical factors for project success.

Success Factors from the Literature	Pinto (1986)	Kerzner (1987)	Pinto & Slevin (1989)	Belassi & Tukel (1996)	Wateridge (1995)	Belout (1998)	Clarke (1999)	Cooke-Daview (2002)	Muller 2005)
Corporate understanding		X	X		X				
Common understanding with stakeholders on success criteria				X					
Executive commitment	X	X	X		X				
Organizational adaptability		X							
Communication	X		X				X		
Project manager selection criteria	X	X	X		X				X
Project manager leadership/empowerment	X	X	X		X				X
Environment			X						
Commitment to planning and control	X	X	X				X		X
Project mission / common goal / direction	X		X				X	X	
Top management support	X		X		X				
Client consultation / acceptance	X	X	X						
Monitor performance and feedback	X		X					X	X
Personnel / teamwork	X	X	X		X	X		X	X
Technical task ability	X	X	X						
Trouble shooting / risk management	X		X					X	
Project ownership								X	X
Urgency of Project			X		X				
Duration and size of Project					X		X	X	
Remarks: "X" success factor(s) that is determined by the researcher either on a conceptual or empirical basis									

Table 2. Literature Review On Critical Success Factors for Project Success (Kuen et al., 2009)

7 PROJECT IMPLEMENTATION PROFILE

It was Slevin and Pinto (1987) who proposed, Project Implementation Profile (PIP), a scientific basis for success that comprises ten key success factors as project team, client acceptance, communications, client consultation, monitoring and feedback, troubleshooting, project mission, top management support, technical tasks and project schedules/plan. However, this research only identified the critical success factors but did not measure the power of their relationship with project performance.

Pinto and Slevin (1987) classified critical success factors as strategic or tactical. Strategic factors consist of factors such as top management support, project scheduling and project mission, where tactical factors relate to project team and client consultation.

Pinto and Slevin evaluated these ten factors as controllable by the project team. Later they extended the list with four additional factors that are considered as outside the control of project team which were: environmental events, team leader, urgency and power and politics. Various authors in literature have proposed many different critical success factor frameworks and lists, and various researches were done on the relation between specific success factor and project success. The definitions of the ten critical success factors in Project Implementation Profile (PIP) are as follows:

Client Consultation: Client consultation factor is related with project activities that provide the quality of a product (Slevin & Pinto, 1986). Actively listening to all stakeholders, including clients in the implementation process and providing client status reports / communications are parts of the client consultation factor (Slevin & Pinto, 1986). According to PMI, the collection of feedback from the clients and customers throughout the project life cycles increases end product usage and acceptance by the clients.

In PIP questionnaire, the contribution of client consultation factor is measured by the five questions under factor contributions section (Appendix A).

Client Acceptance: Client acceptance is the final step for the implementation of the product and, therefore, it is different from client consultation factor (Slevin & Pinto, 1986). Pinto and Slevin described client acceptance as the attainment of end-user approval and the usage of the end product. According to PMI, the sense of ownership and product acceptance increases as a result of end-user involvement that also improves the perceived project success.

In the questionnaire, the contribution of client acceptance factor is measured by the five questions under factor contributions section (Appendix A).

Communication: Communication is the establishment of necessary communication channels and information flow. According to Slevin and Pinto (1986), communication covers the information flow between team members, clients, organization and related other teams.

In the questionnaire, the effect of communication is measured by the five questions under factor contributions section (Appendix A).

Monitoring and Feedback: Pinto (1986) defined monitoring and feedback as providing full information at milestones throughout the project cycle for project stakeholders. PMI (2008) describes the guidelines related to the monitoring and control activity category. This category covers details about the process improvement evaluations along with risk identification by using forecasting reports and project status reports.

In PIP questionnaire, the contribution of monitoring and feedback factor is measured by the five questions under factor contributions section (Appendix A).

Project Mission: PMI states that project mission success factor involves setting up goals, clearly definition of directions and project objectives to project all stakeholders. According to PMI, the project charter is used in the establishment of the project scope statement in order to define the product characteristics that will be delivered by the project team members. The scope statement describes the extent of product functionality, the overall project objectives and establishment of the project scope. It is broken down into smaller tasks in order to accomplish the aimed product.

In Project Implementation Profile questionnaire, the effect of project mission factor is measured the five questions under factor contributions section (Appendix A).

Project Schedule / Plan: Slevin & Pinto (1986) described the project schedule factor as forming the detailed task requirements necessary for the implementation of a project. The planning category includes activities related to establishing definite goals defined for project resources such as creating a work breakdown structure. According to PMI, the structure is a hierarchy of required tasks to accomplish the deliverables of the project. These deliverables sum is the product delivery that provides an aimed benefit to stakeholders.

In the questionnaire, the contribution of "project schedule/plan" factor is measured by the five questions under factor contributions section (Appendix A).

Project Team: Project team factor is associated with training, selecting, and recruiting project team members in order them to participate in the best way in related project tasks (Slevin & Pinto, 1986). According to PMI, human resource planning includes the development of a staffing plan in order to fill needed positions by analyzing the roles that are needed to do the project tasks.

In the questionnaire, the contribution of project team is measured by the five questions under factor contributions section (Appendix A).

Technical Tasks: The technical tasks factor includes activities that are related to accomplish technical objectives by ensuring the availability of the related procedures, technology and resources (Slevin & Pinto, 1986). PMI describes the planning activities as the process to decide which, how and when to acquire the necessary technology and resources.

In the questionnaire, the effect of technical task is measured by the five questions under factor contributions section (Appendix A).

Top Management Support: According to PMI, management support is executive management's readiness for delegating and authorizingpower to provide the necessary resources for the project. PMI supports this factor as a CSF by sharing the activity as a best practice in the PMBOK. PMI documents the initiating group containing the project charter document as a formal deliverable which is published by the project sponsor. The project sponsor authorizes resource expenditure and the project's existence.

In the questionnaire, the contribution of management support factor is measured by the five questions under factor contributions section (Appendix A).

Troubleshooting: This factor involves team members to recognize that usually problems arise with projects, regardless of how careful planning is done. Therefore, project team members should make necessary amendments to handle the unexpected situations from the plan (Slevin & Pinto, 1986). As Pinto (1986) pointed out successful project teams make arrangements to manage, foresee problems and prevent issues during the life cycle of the project. In PMBOK the monitor and control category includes details on processes to oversee execution, recognize potential issues and initiate corrective actions.

In PIP, the effect of troubleshooting is measured by the five questions under factor contributions section (Appendix A).

Table 3 presents the importance rankings of critical success factors in various studies according to the Project Implementation Profile. In the ranking, "1" represents the most important and "10" represents the least important factor. As we see, there were differences in findings between each study.

	Hyvari (2006)	Finch (2003)	Delisle & Thomas (2002)	Pinto & Presscott (1988)	Pinto & Slevin (1987)
Project Mission	6	7	1	1	1
Top Management Support	4	6	9	7	2
Project Schedule/Plans	5	5	5	9	9
Client Consultation	2	1	2	2	4
Personnel (Project Team)	9	10	10	10	5
Technical Task	7	9	4	3	6
Client Acceptance	3	4	6	4	7
Monitoring and Feedback	10	3	3	5	8
Communication	1	2	8	6	9
Trouble-shooting	7	8	7	8	10

Table 3: Project Implementation Profile CSF Importance Rankings (Hyvari, 2006)

8 PROPOSED RESEARCH MODEL AND HYPOTHESES

The initial aim of this study is:

- To implement Project Implementation Profile (PIP) instrument, developed by Slevin and Pinto (1986), in order to collect data for project success criteria and critical success factors,

- To statistically analyze the thirteen project success criteria in order to discover the project success understanding in IT sector.

- To statistically analyze the relationship between ten critical success factors and IT project performance.

- To examine the moderating effect of project duration, and organization structure on the relationship between project management critical success factors and project performance in IT sector.

Thus, the study attempts to concentrate on the following research questions that need further analysis.

1. How project performance is measured and what are the most important success criteria in IT area?

2. Which critical success factors affect the project success in IT sector?

3. Is there a significant relationship between information technology project performance and the critical success factors in information technology market?

4. What is the moderating effect of project duration on the relationship between project management success factors and project performance in information technology sector?

5. What is the moderating effect of organization structure on the relationship between project management success factors and project performance in information technology sector?

The independent variables, identified as critical success factors by Slevin and Pinto (1986) are Communications, Client Consultation, Personnel (Project Team), Client Acceptance, Project Mission, Monitoring and Feedback, Project Schedule or Plan, Technical Tasks, Troubleshooting and Top Management Support. These factors established by Pinto (1986) and Slevin & Pinto (1986) were measured by the Project Implementation Profile (PIP) instrument.

As many researchers used PIP instrument to collect data (Pinto & Prescott, 1988; Pinto & Slevin, 1989; Delisle, 2001; Finch, 2003; Jones, 2007; Culler, 2009), the same instrument is used for this research. The data will be used for statistical analysis to analyze the relationship between critical success factors and information technology project performance.

In addition to Project Implementation Profile questionnaire, two additional moderating factors below are included in the model: project duration and organization structure.

Project Duration: Project duration is the time frame between project initiation and closure phases. Cooke and Daview (2002) and Wateridge (1995) identified schedule duration as a critical factor.

Organization Structure: In this study, the use of different types of organizations and their effectiveness in project management will be examined. The respondents will be asked to select the organization type that best describe their organization structure. The definitions that will be used are functional, weak matrix, strong matrix and projectized.

The dependent variable is project performance. Project success will be measured by a response from the participant about whether the project he/she selected was unsuccessful or successful. The response is referred to as project success perception. The twelve statements (success criteria) related to elements of project outcome analyzed by Slevin and Pinto (1986) also measured project performance in a more objective way. The average of scaled scores of the twelve statements will be referred to as project performance in the research study. The twelve project success statements and questions exist under project performance criteria section of the questionnaire (Appendix A). The definitions of the statements are as follows:

1. On Schedule: The project is completed within schedule.

2. On Budget: The project is completed within budget.

3. Benefit the Users: The output of the project is for the benefit of the users in terms of efficiency and effectiveness.

4. Best Solution: The output of the project is the best solution for the request or problem of the client.

5. Important Clients Make Use of: Important clients – project sponsors – use and satisfied from the output of the project.

6. Increases User Effectiveness: The output of the project increases the decision making effectiveness of the users.

7. Minimum Problems: The output of the project is accepted by the users and initial non-technical problems are minimal.

8. Product is Used: The output of the project is used by the estimated users.

9. Product Works: The output of the project works.

10. Team Satisfaction: The project team is satisfied to take part in the project.

11. Performance Improvement: The output of the project improves the operations / processes of the target population.

12. Positive Impact: The output of the project has a positive effect on users.

13. Success Perception: Regardless of the twelve performance questions, what the project team member thinks about the success of the project.

Figure 1: Proposed Research Model

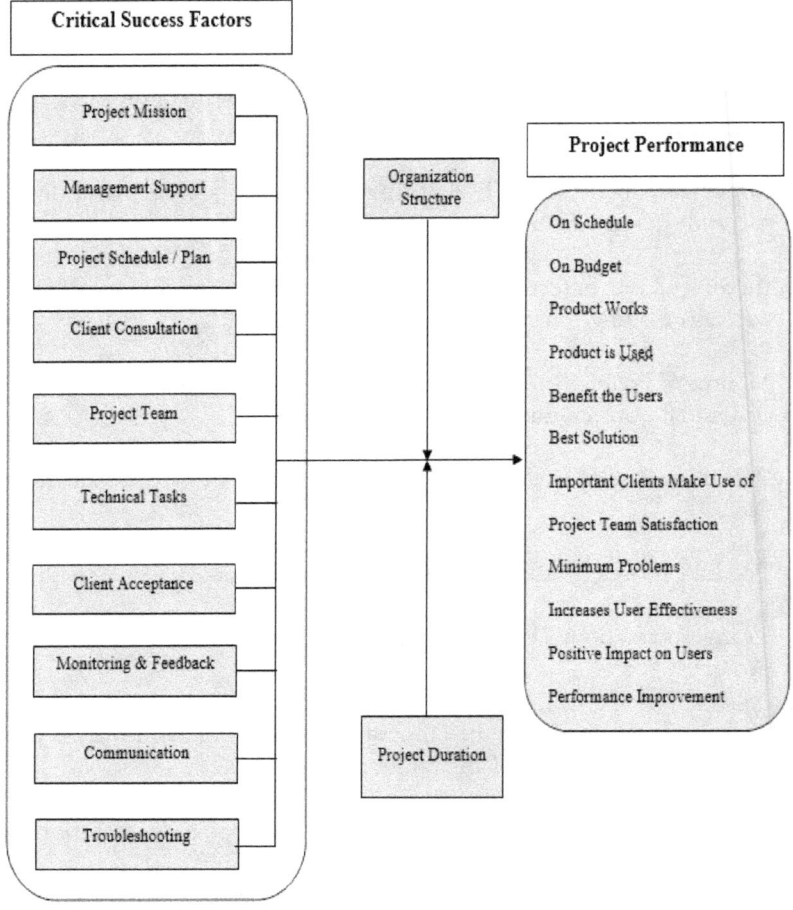

Hypotheses illustrate the possible outcomes based on research questions in a study (Neuman, 2003; Creswell, 2005). The hypotheses for the research study are as follows:

Hypothesis H1: A clear project mission will have a positive influence on project performance and explains the variance in it.

Hypothesis H2: High support from the top management will have a positive influence on project performance and explains the variance in it.

Hypothesis H3: A detailed project schedule/plan will have a positive influence on project performance and explains the variance in it.

Hypothesis H4: Frequent and high client consultation will have a positive influence on project performance and explains the variance in it.

Hypothesis H5: Competent project team will have a positive influence on project performance and explains the variance in it.

Hypothesis H6: The availability of technical tasks force will have a positive influence on project performance and explains the variance in it.

Hypothesis H7: High client acceptance will have a positive influence on project performance and explains the variance in it.

Hypothesis H8: Frequent monitoring and feedback activity will have a positive influence on project performance and explains the variance in it.

Hypothesis H9: Effective and sufficient communication will have a positive influence on project performance and explains the variance in it.

Hypothesis H10: Capability in trouble-shooting will have a positive influence on project performance and explains the variance in it.

Hypothesis H11: Project duration will moderate the relationship between project mission and project performance.

Hypothesis H12: Organization structure will moderate the relationship between client consultation and project success.

9 RESEARCH DESIGN AND METHODOLOGY

Meredith et. al. (1989) establishes the framework for operations research. Two dimensions are used: Existential / Rational and Artificial / Natural.

Rationalism uses pure logic and a formal structure as the final measure of truth. Existentialism is the attitude that knowledge is received through human process of interacting with the environment. The two dimensions involve four perspectives: logical positivist/empiricist, axiomatic, critical theory and interpretive. In the research methodology, this study takes the logical positivist/empiricist approach.

The second dimension of the framework is natural dimension / artificial. It relates to the information and source used in the study. The two dimensions include three perspectives: artificial reconstruction of object reality, people's perceptions of object reality and direct observation of object reality. The study will be based on perceptions of people about the concepts.

Meredith et. al. (1989) suggests surveys and structured interviewing in order to use the people's perceptions of object reality for the logical positivist/empiricist approach. Therefore, surveys will be used as a data collection method for this research.

In this study, quantitative hypothesis-testing research method has been used. As this research initially plans to study whether are there any relationships between critical success factors (independent variables) and information technology project performance (dependent variables) and the effect on relationships, after controlling data for project duration and organization (moderating variables), the design of the study is explanatory.

The unit of analysis of this research was project member. Since a project member may work on more than one project at the same time in; the target population was especially asked to cover only the latest completed information technology projects.

The survey was delivered through Project Management Institute

Turkey (has more than 500 members), Istanbul Project Management Association (has more than 500 members), Informatics Association of Turkey (has more than 10,000 members) and professional network.

Data was collected using Project Implementation Profile (PIP) Instrument (Appendix A), developed by Slevin and Pinto (1986, 1987). The instrument has been used in several empirical research studies to measure project performance and the contributing factors (Delisle, 2001; Finch, 2003; Hyväri, 2006; Jones, 2007).

The Project Implementation Profile includes declarative statements about dependent and independent variables with a 7-point Likert-type scale option for participants to indicate degree of agreement with each statement. Each participant was asked to respond to survey statements about a completed project only.

The independent variables – critical success factors – are client acceptance, client communication, consultation, monitoring and feedback, project mission, project schedules/plan, project team, technical tasks, top management support and troubleshooting. The dependent variable is project performance. It is measured by the response from the participant about whether the project he/she selected was unsuccessful or successful. The response is referred to as project success perception. The twelve statements (success criteria) related to elements of project outcome analyzed by Slevin and Pinto (1986) also measured project performance. The average of scaled scores of the twelve statements will be referred to as project performance in a more objective way. The project success statements and questions are as follows: on schedule, on budget, benefit the users, best solution, important clients make use of, increases user effectiveness, minimum problems, product is used, product works, performance improvement, positive impact and team satisfaction.

Statistical analysis was used in the current study to quantify the degree of relationship between information technology project performance measured on a 7-point Likert-type scale and critical success factors measured on a 7-point Likert-type scale (Likert, 1932). The Likert-type scale was used in survey instruments. According to DeVellis (2003), participants were informed to respond to a declarative statement by selecting a response option expressing a degree of agreement with the statement.

Considering that the sampling frame of this research is information technology area projects, necessary institutions to reach the sector was defined. A presentation was formed in order to explain the purpose of this research and potential benefits for the sector. The presentation was sent to management of Project Management Institute Turkey, Istanbul Project Management Institute and Informatics Association of Turkey, prior to necessary phone calls explaining the purpose of the research. Also, support was asked from information technology heads of banking, finance and telecommunication companies, through professional network.

The questionnaire was prepared by online survey application Survey Monkey (www.surveymonkey.com). After necessary approvals had been granted, it was sent to relevant professional institutions, associations and professional network.

Before sending automatically generated electronic mails, the management of the professional institutions and companies sent separate electronic mails to their organizations explaining the study and asking their support. The same electronic mails, with the given approval of the institutions and companies, were sent three times to the ones who did not reply, as a reminder.

The data collection process took place in 2014. The questionnaire forms were distributed electronically to the members of related associations, Project Management Institute Turkey, Istanbul Project Management Institute, Informatics Association of Turkey and other IT companies in professional network.

10 RESEARCH FINDINGS

The aim of this chapter is to present and discuss the research results. The data was gathered through the questionnaire from online survey site, surveymonkey.com. PMI Turkey Chapter, Istanbul Project Management Association and Informatics Association of Turkey provided support with the administration of questionnaire by sending the survey link to their email lists. Also, online community groups associated with project management profession were reached through network platforms LinkedIn.com and Facebook.com.

Association / LinkedIn Community	Number of Members/Registered Participants
PMI Turkey Chapter	500
Istanbul Project Management Association	500
Informatics Association of Turkey	10,000
LinkedIn - PMO Turkey	706
LinkedIn – IT & Telecom Turkey	1,446
LinkedIn - Turk IT	8,828
TOTAL	21,980

Table 4. Survey Associations and Online Communities

10.1. Demographic Results

The survey measured demographic items, with optional questions, such as gender, age, education degree, job experience, project role and core business of the company.

When we look at the gender of 326 participants, 38% (125) of them were female and 62% (201) of them were male. The average age of 324 respondents was 36, showing us that the participants of the survey were generally senior IT professionals.

The participants were well educated related to information technology sector needs: Of the 329 respondents, 6% (20) had high school, 61% (200) had undergraduate, 30% (99) had graduate and 3% (10) had Ph.D. degrees (Figure 2).

The participants were experienced IT professionals. Only 4% (12) participants had less than one year experience and 17% (56) had up to 5 years of experience. The majority of participants, 25% (81), were on the field for 6 to 10 years, where 22% (74) were for 11 to 15 years. The more senior participants had for 16 to 20 years experience, 18% (60), and 14% (46) have more than 20 years of experience. In total of 329 participants, about 79% (261) had more than 5 years of experience (Figure 3).

Figure 2. Education Degree

Education Degree

Figure 3. Job Experience

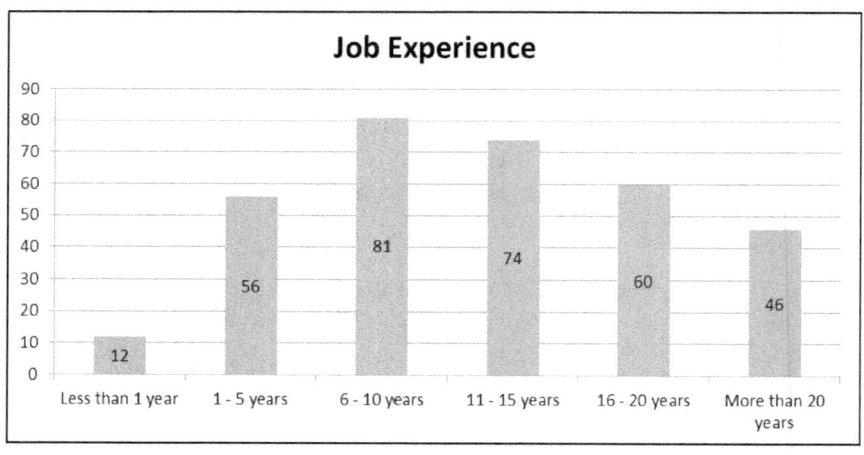

Of the 319 respondents, 50% (159) of them were project team members, 19% (60) of them were resource managers or team leaders, 29% (93) of them were project managers or project leaders and finally 2% (7) of them were project sponsors (Figure 4).

The participants of the survey were working in different sectors. Most of the respondents were working for finance/banking/insurance sectors (60%, 197 participants), 21% (68) were working for software industry, 10% (32) of the respondents were from other sectors (government, health care, insurance, etc), 5% (15) were working for telecommunications sector and finally 4% (12) were for other service and engineering sectors (Figure 5).

Figure 4. Project Role

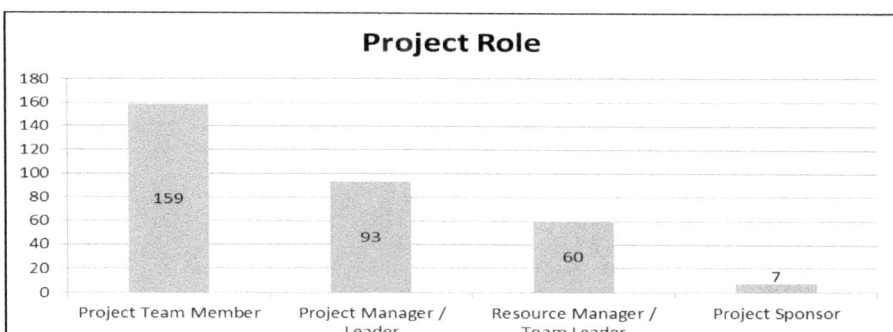

Figure 5. Sector Information

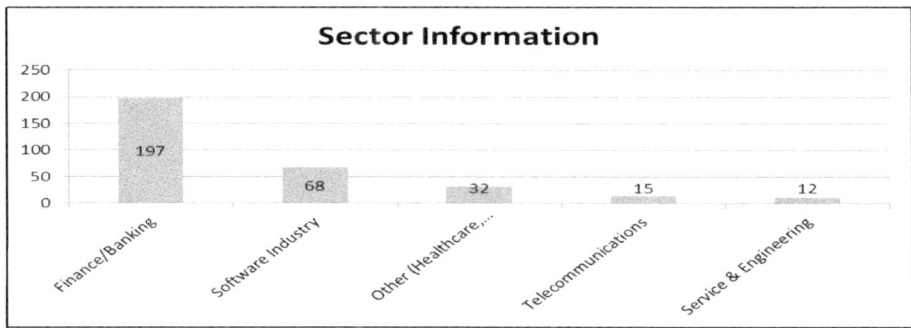

10.2. Project Based Data

When we look at the project team sizes, 27% (73) of teams had up to 10 members. The majority of the teams – 34% (90) – had 11 to 20 members. Other results were as follows: 13% (34) had 21 to 30 members, 5% (13) had 31 to 40 members, 7% (18) had 41 to 50 members, 7% (19) had 51 to 100 members and 6% (17) had more than 100 members (Figure 6).

Figure 6. Project Team Sizes

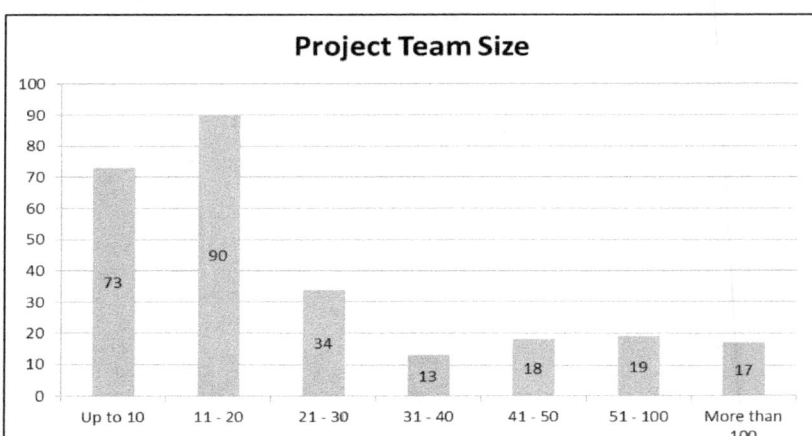

The organization structures of participants' companies were various. According to the survey, the least preferred organization structure was functional organizations where there were only team leaders / resource managers, 8% (21). Weak matrix organization structures, where main decisions were given by team leaders / resource managers instead of project managers preferred by 20% (52). Strong matrix organizations, where project managers / leaders and team leaders / resource managers share authority equally were the most preferred organization structure, 56% (148). Project based organization structure, where project managers had the biggest authority, were 16% (43) (Figure 7).

Figure 7. Organization Structure

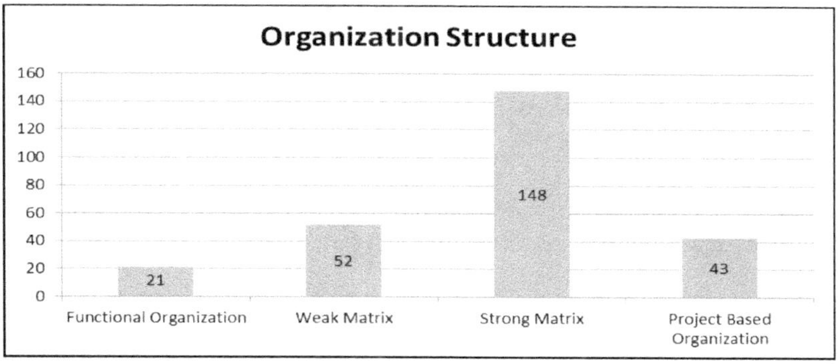

Finally, the average information technology project duration in Turkey was 9 months, related to 264 answers coming from participants.

10.3. Project Success Criteria

As mentioned before, there is no general agreement on project success criteria. Therefore, it is hard to talk about complete success, so instead we mostly talk about perceived or subjective success that changes for each stakeholder.

In our research, to overcome this subjective understanding of success, as we have mentioned, we used project success criteria of project implementation profile (PIP). In this method, we asked 13 questions to participants in order to measure project success. In these questions, 12 of them were about project criteria with absolute answers, while the final question had a subjective answer. For, all answers "Agree" and "Strongly Agree" were considered as positive answers, while "Strongly Disagree", "Disagree", "Somewhat Disagree", "Neutral" and "Somewhat Agree" were considered as negative answers.

The first criteria was about schedule and the question was "This project finished on schedule or not." 107 of the 233 participants chose "Agree" or "Strongly Agree." This means in Turkish IT sector 54% of the projects finished on time, while 46% of them finish with some delay.

The second criteria was about cost control and when we asked the participants, "This project came in on budget or not", 98 of the 233 participants chose "Agree" or "Strongly Agree" options.

As a result it was seen that only 42% of the projects finished in their budget, while 58% exceeded their current budget, in Turkish IT sector that represented in our survey.

When we asked the participants, "The project that has been developed worked or not", as the third criteria, 181 of the 233 participants chose "Agree" or "Strongly Agree." This means that 78% of the end products worked properly, while only 22% of the end products of the projects did not work as it initially planned.

In order to measure customer satisfaction as the fourth criteria, we asked the participants, "The project was used by its intended clients or not." As a result, 206 of the 233 participants agreed or strongly agreed that meant 88% of the customers were using the related products.

For measuring the effect of the product we asked the participants, "This project directly benefitted the intended users: either through increasing efficiency / employee effectiveness or not", 174 of the 233 participants chose "Agree" or "Strongly Agree" which meant 75% of the participants found the end product useful.

The sixth criterion was about the quality of the solution that the specific project served: "Given the problem for which it was developed, this project seems to do the best job of solving the problem, i.e., it was the best choice among the set of alternatives." 149 of the 233 participants agreed or strongly agreed that meant 64% of participants were satisfied with the solution.

The seventh criteria tried to measure the effect of the project on important clients, "Important clients, directly affected by this project, will make use of it." Related to this question 183 of the 233 participants said they agreed or strongly agreed about the final output on important clients, that was 79%.

After asking about other criteria, the participants were asked how they felt about the project development process as a team member: "I was satisfied with the process by which this project was completed." Related to the answers, 131 of the 233 participants - 56% - were satisfied about the project development process.

We took the opinion of participants about the quality of the specific project with the criterion: "We are confident that non-technical start-up problems will be minimal, because the project will be readily accepted by its intended users." About, 123 of the 233 participants, approximately 53%, agreed/strongly agreed about the quality of the project.

The tenth success criterion was again about the positive business effect of the project: "Use of this project has directly lead to be improved or more effective decision making or performance for the clients." When we looked at the answers, 138 of the 233 participants - 59% - agreed or strongly agreed to this proposition.

Another success criterion about business effect was, "This project will have a positive effect on those who make use of it." Related to the results, 173 of the 233 participants, 74%, said they agreed or strongly agreed about the positive impact of the end product.

The last specific criterion was about operational efficiency, "The results of this project represent a definite improvement in performance over the way clients used to perform these activities." 69% of participants – 161 of 233 - believed that the end product improved operational efficiency.

Finally, other than all specific success criteria, how did the participants generally evaluate the success of the project was the last criterion: "All things considered, this project was/will be a success." Related to answers, 77% of participants – 180 of 233 – "agree" or "strongly agree" that their project was successful.

As a result, when we look at the classical project management success criteria - Cost, Quality and Schedule – we see that these success rates were quite low, by 42%, 53% and 54% respectively, which were parallel to other international research results. Also, project team satisfaction was quite low with 56%. On the other hand, end product success results were better, ranging from 59% to 88%, with an average of 73%.

When we took the average of 12 specific success criteria, average project success rate was calculated as 66%. On the other hand, away from specific criteria, perceived success of projects related to participants were 77%, better than the average of 12 specific criteria (Figure 8).

Figure 8: Success Rates Based on Success Criteria

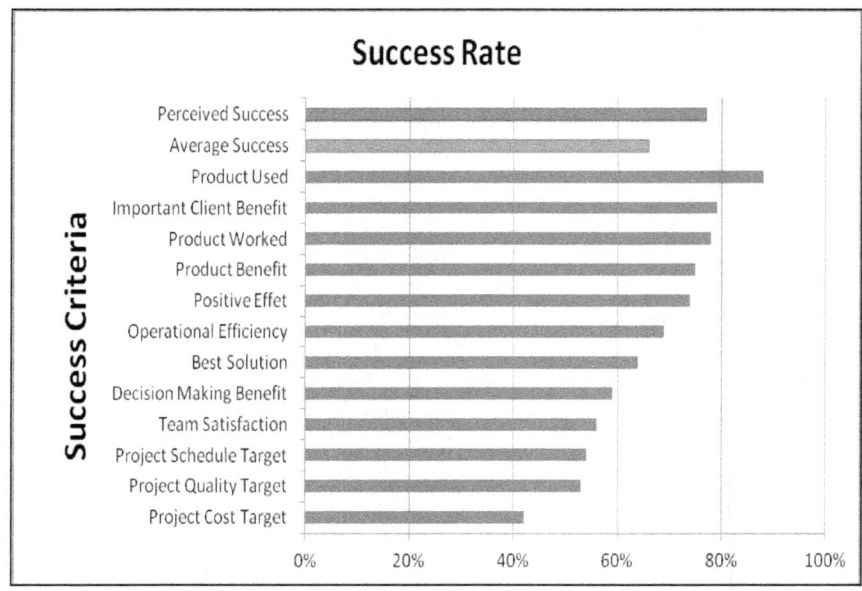

In our research, we took the average success, the average result of 12 specific success rates, as the project performance for future analysis.

10.4. Factor Analysis

Factor analysis is performed to reduce a very large of number of variables to a manageable, meaningful and explainable set of factors. A principal-component analysis (PCA) converts all the variables into a set of combined variables that are not correlated to one another (Sekaran, 2003). Therefore, in this study, PCA is done to find out how many different dimensions the respondents recognize and whether they feel them the same as in the original data with which the scale was developed.

PCA involves a mathematical procedure that decreases the number of correlated variables into a lower number of uncorrelated variables (principal components). Principal component analysis is useful when you have obtained data on a large number of variables and believe that there is some repetition - variables are correlated with one another - in those variables. Based on this repetition, it is attainable to reduce the observed variables into a lower number of artificial variables. These variables - principal components - will explain of the variance and fluctuations in the observed variables. The methods in that group are used for deciding the validity of the factor model that is predefined and predetermined. Stages of Principal Components Analysis are "Kaiser-Meyer-Olkin Sampling Adequacy Coefficient" (KMO) and "Bartlett Test of Sphericity." The KMO measure of sampling adequacy tests whether the partial correlations among variables are small. According to Hair et al. (2006), the lower limit for KMO that is agreed upon is 0.50.

If there is heterogeneity of the data set, there are two ways to reach homogeneity. The sample size can be increased or the variables that have negative kurtosis or are extremely skewed can be neglected one by one by using quantitative data analysis method.

According to Hair et al. (2006), Bartlett's test gives the statistical significance of the inter-correlation between variable and the upper limit for the value of p in Social Sciences that is agreed upon is 0.05.

After running the PCA for our model, KMO sampling adequacy coefficient was calculated as 0.930 which was greater than 0.5. Since KMO was also greater than 0.8, this showed that variables were perfectly appropriate for factor analysis (Durmuş et al. 2011). Barlett's significance was 0.00, which was under 0.005, showed that our variables were appropriate for analysis.

In order to construct the table for the results of PCA first we looked at "Total Variance Explained" table to determine the significant components. That meant their total "Initial Eigen Values" were greater than 1. In our study we had 9 components whose totals were greater than 1, measuring %73.442 of the total variance.

From the "Rotated Component Matrix" we included each variable to the component that had the absolute value greater than 0.5. As a result of the factor analysis, we formed a "factor analysis result table" with nine components: 1) Monitoring, Feedback and Communication, 2) Project Planning, 3) Client Consultation, 4) Management Support, 5) Technical Tasks, 6) Project Mission, 7) Client Acceptance, 8) Troubleshooting and 9) Troubleshooting Support (Project Success Factors Factor Analysis Result Table).

The component table was a little different from the existing component structure of Project Implementation Profile (PIP) survey. We saw that although there were ten components in the original PIP survey, in our research we determined nine components related to survey answers:

"Monitoring and Feedback" and "Communication" variables were grouped together under "Monitoring, Feedback and Communication" component. This was because for project management "monitoring and feedback" was a part of "communication" function. Also, "Project Schedule" and "Project Team" components were grouped together forming one component as "Project Planning." Project planning component involved availability of the necessary human resources for the necessary time. On the other hand, "Troubleshooting" component was divided into two separate components. The first component was about the actions of the project team, the second was about the support that the project team should take outside the team.

10.5. Reliability Analysis

According to Sekaran (2003) the reliability of a measure shows the extent to which it is proper (error free) and for that reason assures consistent measurement across time and across the different times in the instrument. Therefore, the reliability of a measure is an explanation and evidence of the consistency and stability with which the instrument measures the approach and supports to determine the goodness of a measure.

The ability of a measure to continue to be the same over time – despite uncontrollable testing environment or the state of the respondents – is the characteristic of its stability and low vulnerability to changes in the environment.

The internal consistency of measures shows the homogeneity of the items in the measure. The items should be together as a set and be capable of measuring the same idea separately so that the respondents link the same meaning to each of the items. This can be seen by analyzing if the items in the measuring instrument are correlated highly or not. The most significant test of consistency reliability is the Cronbach's coefficient alpha that is used for multi-scaled items. Where the coefficients are higher the measuring instrument is better (Sekaran, 2003). Durmuş et al. (2011) states that Cronbach alpha should be greater than or equal to 0.70. If it's below 0.70, items are eliminated from the instrument until the coefficient reaches 0.70. If there are two items under an inconsistent instrument, the one having the higher relation to the core concept is kept in the model, the other is eliminated.

Reliability Analysis of Monitoring, Feedback and Communication

Our first factor, monitoring, feedback and communication, consisted of ten questions. The cronbach alpha of the factor – Monitoring - was 0.958, which showed that this factor was reliable.

Reliability Analysis of Project Planning

The project planning factor consisted of eight questions. The cronbach alpha of this factor was 0.904, which showed that it was reliable.

Reliability Analysis of Client Consultation

Our third factor, client consultation, consisted of five questions. The cronbach alpha of the factor was 0.938, which showed that this factor was reliable.

Reliability Analysis of Management Support

The fourth factor, management support, consisted of five questions. The cronbach alpha of our factor was 0.893, which showed that this factor was reliable.

Reliability Analysis of Technical Tasks

Our fifth factor, technical tasks, consisted of five questions. The cronbach alpha of the factor was 0.860, which showed that this factor was reliable.

Reliability Analysis of Project Mission

Project Mission consisted of five questions. The cronbach alpha of the factor was 0.856, which showed that this factor was reliable.

Reliability Analysis of Client Acceptance

Client Acceptance consisted of four questions. The details of reliability analysis were shown below. The cronbach alpha of our factor was 0.804, which showed that this factor was reliable.

Reliability Analysis of Troubleshooting

Troubleshooting consisted of three questions. The cronbach alpha was 0.807, which showed the factor was reliable.

Reliability Analysis of Troubleshooting Support

The last factor, troubleshooting support consisted of two questions. The cronbach alpha of the factor was 0.741, which showed that this factor was reliable.

The proposed research model was based on existing theories, where Project Implementation Profile (PIP) was used as mentioned in literature review. Related to this information, principle component analysis was accomplished just as a supplementary work in this study. As a result, research studies were carried on by using PIP survey, after implementing reliability and multicolinearity analysis in order to check and be sure for the reliability of the model.

10.6. Reliability Analysis for PIP Project Success Factors

Reliability Analysis of Project Mission

As all in PIP project success factors project mission consisted of five questions. The cronbach alpha of the factor was 0.856, which showed that this factor was reliable.

Reliability Analysis of Management Support

Management Support factor consisted of five questions. The cronbach alpha of the factor was 0.893, which showed that this factor was reliable.

Reliability Analysis of Project Schedule/Plan

Project Schedule / Plan consisted of five questions. The cronbach alpha of the factor was 0.849, which showed that this factor was reliable.

Reliability Analysis of Client Consultation

As all in PIP project success factors client consultation consisted of five questions. The cronbach alpha of the factor was 0.938, which showed that this factor was reliable.

Reliability Analysis of Project Team

As other PIP project success factors project team consisted of five questions. The cronbach alpha of the factor was 0.829, which showed that this factor was reliable.

Reliability Analysis of Technical Tasks

Technical tasks consisted of five questions. The cronbach alpha of the factor was 0.867, which showed that this factor was reliable.

Reliability Analysis of Client Acceptance

Client acceptance consisted of five questions. The cronbach alpha of the factor was 0.807, which showed that this factor was reliable.

Reliability Analysis of Monitoring and Feedback

Monitoring and feedback consisted of five questions. The cronbach alpha of the factor was 0.807, which showed that this factor was reliable.

Reliability Analysis of Communication

Communication consisted of five questions. The cronbach alpha of the factor was 0.936, which showed that this factor was reliable.

Reliability Analysis of Troubleshooting

Troubleshooting consisted of five questions. The cronbach alpha of the factor was 0.818, which showed that this factor was reliable.

As a result, we can say that all project success factors that were part of Project Implementation Profile survey were reliable.

10.7. Hypothesis Testing

Regression and Correlation Analysis

Multiple regression analysis specifies the power of relationship between independent variables and the dependent variable. It's the mathematical declaration of the relation. Durmuş et al. (2011) explains the stages of multiple regression and correlation analysis as follows:

- Linearity: It means that the relationship between an independent variable and the dependent variable is greater than or equal to 0.70. If the relationship is below 0.70, that independent variable is eliminated from the model.

- Multicolinearity: It is a problem case that there exists a relationship between independent variables. Whenever the relationship between any independent variables is greater than 0.70, there two variables are dependent to each other. If there is a relationship between two independent variables, the variable whose relationship with the dependent variable is lower is eliminated from the model.

- Exploratory Power of the model and its validity: Exploratory power of the model is measured by adjusted r square. If r2 is greater than 0.49, the model is powerful. Total validity of the model is measured by F test. If F test result is significant, the model is valid.

- Contribution of external variable to the exploratory power of the model: Insignificant Betas are eliminated by applying T test.

In order to eliminate multicolinearity, correlation analysis was made and independent variables whose relations were greater than 0.7 were identified. Those variables were: Project Planning, Project Team, Communication, Monitoring and Feedback.

Multiple Regression Analysis

Multiple regression analysis was performed to obtain a valid model explaining the relationship between PIP project success factors and project success. We eliminated variables that caused multicollineratiy with each other.

First we eliminated Project Team and Communication from the model and made multiple regression analysis.

When we check F-Test from Anova Table, we saw that our model was significant for predictors, project mission, technical tasks and client consultation:
Sig = 0.000<0.05 (Model is Significant)

For T test and β coefficients we looked at coefficients table and determined that Technical Tasks, Project Mission and Client Consultation independent variables were significant:

Technical Tasks Sig.   = 0.000 < 0.05 (Significant)
Project Mission Sig   = 0.000 < 0.05 (Significant)
Client Consultation Sig   = 0.001 < 0.05 (Significant)

The VIF value of independent variables was below 10 showing that there was no multicolineratiy between variables.

In the model summary, we saw that our Adjusted R Square value was 0.679. Since this value was greater than 0.50 we said that explanatory power of our model was good:

Adjusted R Square = 0.679 > 0.50 (explanatory value of the model was good).

When we looked at the standard coefficients, in the independent variables, project mission (0.412), technical tasks (0.405) and client consultation (0.168) explained project performance.

As reflected on above, Project Mission, Technical Tasks and Client Consultation had positive contribution on Project Performance. The overall explanatory power of model was 68% (R=0.827; R2=0.684; F=127.119, p=0.000).

Figure 9.   Regressions for Project Mission, Technical Tasks, Client
Consultation and Project Performance

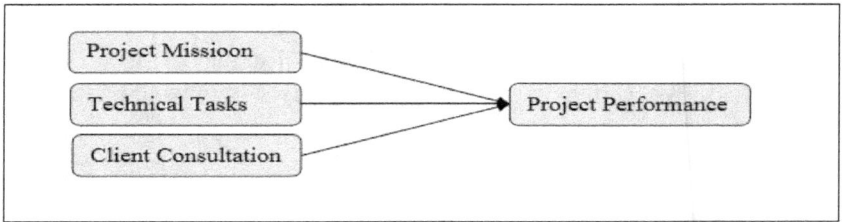

For the second analysis, we eliminated project plan and communication from the model and made multiple regression analysis.

In Anova Table, we saw that our model was significant for predictors, project mission, technical tasks and client consultation:
Sig = 0.000<0.05 (Model is Significant)

For T test and β coefficients we looked at coefficients table and determined that technical tasks, project mission and client consultation independent variables were significant:

Technical Tasks Sig.   = 0.000 < 0.05 (Significant)
Project Mission Sig   = 0.000 < 0.05 (Significant)
Client Consultation Sig   = 0.001 < 0.05 (Significant)

The VIF value of independent variables was below 10 showing that there was no multicolineratiy between variables.

In the Model Summary Table, we saw that our Adjusted R Square value was 0.679. Since this value was greater than 0.50 we said that explanatory power of our model was good:

Adjusted R Square = 0.679 > 0.50 (explanatory value of the model was good).

When we looked at the standard coefficients, in the independent variables, project mission (0.412), technical tasks (0.405) and client consultation (0.168) explained project performance.

For the third analysis, we eliminated project plan and monitoring & feedback from the model and made multiple regression analysis.

In Anova Table, we saw that our model was significant for predictors, project mission, technical tasks and client consultation:
Sig = 0.000<0.05 (Model is Significant)

For T test and β coefficients we looked at coefficients table and determined that Technical Tasks, Project Mission and Client Consultation independent variables were significant:

Technical Tasks Sig.　　　　= 0.000 < 0.05 (Significant)
Project Mission Sig　　　　　= 0.000 < 0.05 (Significant)
Client Consultation Sig　　　= 0.001 < 0.05 (Significant)

The VIF value of independent variables was below 10 showing that there was no multicolineratiy between variables.

In the Model Summary Table, we saw that our Adjusted R Square value was 0.679. Since this value was greater than 0.50 we said that explanatory power of our model was good:

Adjusted R Square = 0.679 > 0.50 (explanatory value of the model was good).

When we looked at the standard coefficients, in the independent variables, project mission (0.412), technical tasks (0.405) and client consultation (0.168) explained project performance.

For the fourth analysis, we eliminated project team and monitoring & feedback from the model and made multiple regression analysis.

In Anova Table, we saw that our model was significant for predictors, project mission, technical tasks and client consultation:
Sig = 0.000<0.05 (Model is Significant)

For T test and β coefficients we looked at coefficients table and determined that technical tasks, project mission and client consultation independent variables were significant:

Technical Tasks Sig.　　　　= 0.000 < 0.05 (Significant)
Project Mission Sig　　= 0.000 < 0.05 (Significant)
Client Consultation Sig　　　= 0.001 < 0.05 (Significant)

The VIF value of independent variables was below 10 showing that there was no multicolineratiy between variables.

In the Model Summary Table, we saw that our Adjusted R Square value was 0.679. Since this value was greater than 0.50 we said that explanatory power of our model was good:

Adjusted R Square = 0.679 > 0.50 (explanatory value of the model was good).

When we looked at the standard coefficients, in the independent variables, project mission (0.412), technical tasks (0.405) and client consultation (0.168) explained project performance.

Hierarchical Regression Analysis with Project Duration

Hierarchical regression analysis was performed to obtain a valid model explaining the moderating effect of project duration with the project success factors and project performance.

When we checked F-Test from Anova Table, we saw that our model was significant:
Sig = 0.000<0.05 (Model is Significant)

For T test and β coefficients we looked at coefficients table and determined that independent variables were significant.

Project Mission Sig.	= 0.000 < 0.05 (Significant)
Technical Tasks Sig.	= 0.000 < 0.05 (Significant)
Client Consultation Sig.	= 0.000 < 0.05 (Significant)
Project Duration Sig	= 0.000 < 0.05 (Significant)

In the Model Summary Table, we saw that our Adjusted R Square value was 0.703. Since this value was greater than 0.50 we said that explanatory power of our model was good:

Adjusted R Square = 0.703 > 0.50 (explanatory value of the model is good).

When we looked at the standard coefficients, in the independent variables, project mission (0.414), technical tasks (0.359) and client consultation (0.185) explained project performance. Also, project duration negatively affected project performance (-0.165).

As reflected above, project mission, technical tasks and client consultation had positive contribution on project performance where project duration had negative contribution. The overall explanatory power of model was 71% (R=0.843; R2=0.710; F=107.019, p=0.000).

Figure 10. Hierarchical Regression Analyses Results - Project Mission, Technical Tasks, Client Consultation, Project Duration and Project Performance

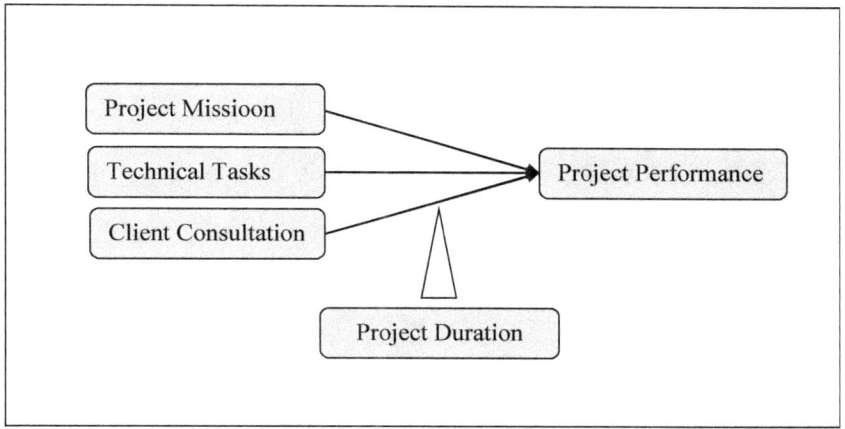

Moderating Effect of Project Organization Structure

When we looked at how organization structure affected project factors, we saw different effects for different organization structures.

For functional organizations, in order to eliminate multicolinearity, correlation analysis was made and independent variables whose relations were greater than 0.7 were identified. Those variables were: Management support, project plan, client consultation, project team, monitoring/feedback and communication.

After we had eliminated variables causing multicollinearity, we looked at the correlation analysis for remaining project success factors.

Project_Performance X Project_Mission = 0.605 < 0.70 (Non-Linear)
Project_Performance X Technical_Tasks = 0.589 < 0.70 (Non-Linear)
Project_Performance X ClientAcceptance= 0.514 < 0.70 (Non-Linear)
Project_Performance X Troubleshooting = 0.892 > 0.70 (Linear)

We found linear relationships between dependent variable project performance and independent variable. This meant that we should go on our analysis with troubleshooting and repeat the regression analysis for this variable.

For troubleshooting, when we checked F-Test from Anova Table, we saw that our model was significant:

Sig = 0.000<0.05 (Model is Significant)

In the Model Summary Table, we saw that our Adjusted R Square value was 0.777. Since this value was greater than 0.50 we said that explanatory power of our model was good:

Adjusted R Square = 0.777 > 0.50 (explanatory value of the model is good).

For T test and β coefficients we looked at Coefficients Table and determined that constant variable was insignificant.

Troubleshooting Sig   = 0.000 < 0.05 (Significant)

When we looked at the standard coefficient, troubleshooting variable explained project performance very well (0.892).

As reflected above, troubleshooting had positive contribution on project performance in functional organizations. The overall explanatory power of the model was 71% (R=0.892; R2=0.796; F=42.929, p=0.000).

Figure 11. Regression Analyses Results in Functional Organizations – Troubleshooting and Project Performance

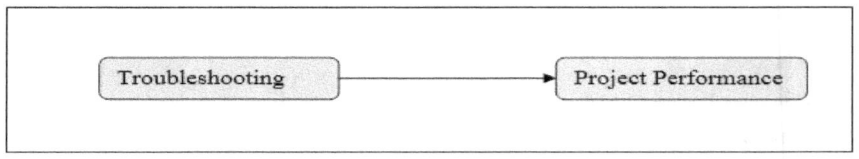

For weak matrix organizations, in order to eliminate multicolinearity, independent variables, whose relations were greater than 0.7 were eliminated from the model. Those variables were: Troubleshooting, project team and monitoring & feedback.

After we had eliminated variables causing multicollinearity, we looked at the correlation analysis for remaining project success factors.

As a result, after eliminating troubleshooting, project team and monitoring & feedback, we looked at the correlation analysis between remaining independent and dependent variables:

Project_Performance X Project_Mission   = 0.655 < 0.70 (Non-Linear)
Project_Performance X Technical Tasks   = 0.759 > 0.70 (Linear)
Project_Performance X Client Acceptance   = 0.426 < 0.70 (Non-Linear)
Project_Performance X Management Support = 0.519 < 0.70 (Non-Linear)
Project_Performance X Project Plan   = 0.341 < 0.70 (Non-Linear)
Project_Performance X Client Consultation   = 0.471 < 0.70 (Non-Linear)
Project_Performance X Communication   = 0.416 < 0.70 (Non-Linear)

We found linear relationship between dependent variable project performance and independent variable technical tasks (0.759). This meant that we should go on our analysis with technical tasks and repeat the regression analysis.

For technical tasks, when we checked F-Test from Anova Table, we saw that our model was significant:
  Sig = 0.000<0.05 (Model is Significant)

In the Model Summary Table, we saw that our Adjusted R Square value was 0.564. Since this value was greater than 0.50 we said that explanatory power of our model was good:

Adjusted R Square = 0.564 > 0.50 (explanatory value of the model is good).

For T test and β coefficients we looked at coefficients table and determined that constant variable was insignificant.

  Technical Tasks Sig   = 0.000 < 0.05 (Significant)

When we looked at the standard coefficient, technical tasks explained project performance very well (0.759).

As reflected on table, technical tasks had positive contribution on project performance in weak matrix organizations. The overall explanatory power of model was 58% (R=0.759; R2=0.577; F=47.659, p=0.000).

Figure 12.　Regression Analysis Results in Weak Matrix Organizations – Technical Tasks and Project Performance

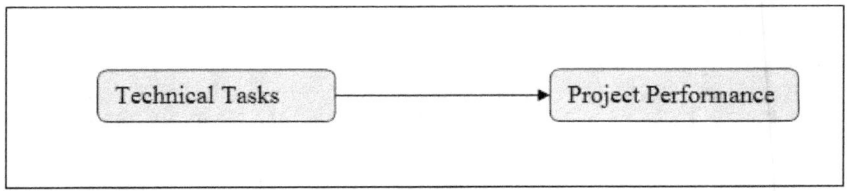

For strong matrix organizations,

In order to eliminate multicolinearity, independent variables, whose relations were greater than 0.7 were eliminated from the model. Those variables were: Communication and Monitoring/Feedback

After we eliminated communication and monitoring/feedback, we looked at the correlation analysis between remaining independent and dependent variables:

Project_Perf.　X Project_Mission　　= 0.755 > 0.70 (Linear)
Project_ Perf.　X Technical_Tasks　= 0.759 > 0.70 (Linear)
Project_ Perf.　X Client _Acceptance　= 0.484 < 0.70 (Non-Linear)
Project_ Perf.　X Project Team　　= 0.569 < 0.70 (Non-Linear)
Project_ Perf.　X Troubleshooting　= 0.489 < 0.70 (Non-Linear)
Project_ Perf.　X Management Support = 0.497 < 0.70 (Non-Linear)
Project_ Perf.　X Project Plan　　= 0.553 < 0.70 (Non-Linear)
Project_ Perf.　X Client Consultation　= 0.545 < 0.70 (Non-Linear)

We found linear relationships between dependent variable project performance and independent variables project mission (0.755) and technical tasks (0.759). We should go on our analysis with project mission and technical tasks and repeat the regression analysis for both of them.

For project mission, when we checked F-Test from Anova Table, we saw that our model was significant:
Sig = 0.000<0.05 (Model is Significant)

In the Model Summary Table, we saw that our Adjusted R Square value was 0.567. Since this value was greater than 0.50 we said that explanatory power of our model was good:

Adjusted R Square = 0.567 > 0.50 (explanatory value of the model is good).

For T test and β coefficients we looked at coefficients table and determined that constant variable was insignificant.

Project Mission Sig = 0.000 < 0.05 (Significant)

When we looked at the standard coefficient, project mission explained project performance very well (0.755).

As reflected above, project mission had positive contribution on project performance in strong matrix organizations. The overall explanatory power of model was 57% (R=0.755; R2=0.571; F=159.396, p=0.000).

For technical tasks, when we checked F-Test from Anova Table, we saw that our model was significant:
Sig = 0.000<0.05 (Model is Significant)

In the Model Summary Table, we saw that our Adjusted R Square value was 0.571. Since this value was greater than 0.50 we said that explanatory power of our model was good:

Adjusted R Square = 0.571 > 0.50 (explanatory value of the model is good).

For T test and β coefficients we looked at coefficients table and determined that constant variable was insignificant.

Technical Tasks Sig = 0.000 < 0.05 (Significant)

When we looked at the standard coefficient, technical tasks explained project performance very well (0.759).

As a result, technical tasks had positive contribution on project performance in strong matrix organizations. The overall explanatory power of model was 58% (R=0.759; R2=0.575; F=149.036, p=0.000).

Figure 13. Regression Analysis Results in Strong Matrix Organizations

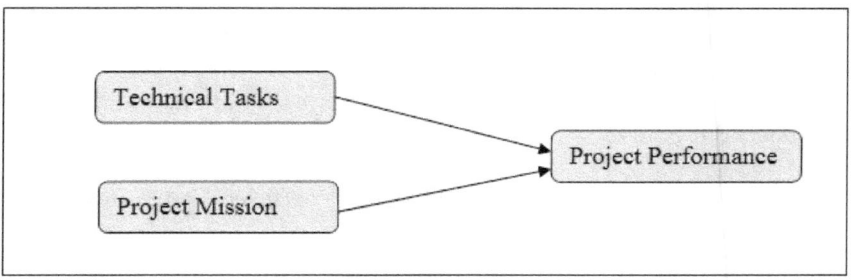

Finally, when we examine project based organizations,

In order to eliminate multicolinearity, independent variables, whose relations were greater than 0.7 were eliminated from the model. Those variables were: Client consultation, project team, communication and troubleshooting.

After we eliminated client consultation, project team, communication and troubleshooting, we looked at the correlation analysis between remaining independent and dependent variables:

Project_ Perf.X Project_Mission = 0.776 > 0.70 (Linear)
Project_Perf. X Management Support = 0.662 < 0.70 (Non-Linear)
Project_ Perf.X Project Plan = 0.534 < 0.70 (Non-Linear)
Project_ Perf.X Technical Tasks = 0.695< 0.70 (Non-Linear)
Project_ Perf.X Client Acceptance = 0.453 < 0.70 (Non-Linear)
Project_ Perf.X Monitoring/Feedback = 0.472 < 0.70 (Non-Linear)

We found linear relationship between dependent variable project performance and independent variable project mission (0.776). This meant that we should go on our analysis with project mission and repeat the regression analysis.

For project mission, when we checked F-Test from Anova Table, we saw that our model was significant:

Sig = 0.000<0.05 (Model is Significant)

In the Model Summary Table, we saw that our Adjusted R Square value was 0.589. Since this value was greater than 0.50 we said that explanatory power of our model was good:

Adjusted R Square = 0.589 > 0.50 (explanatory value of the model is good).

For T test and β coefficients we looked at coefficients table and determined that constant variable was insignificant: Project Mission Sig = 0.000 < 0.05 (Significant)

When we looked at the standard coefficient, project mission explained project performance very well (0.776).

As reflected above, project mission had positive contribution on project performance in projectized organizations. The overall explanatory power of model was 60% (R=0.776; R2=0.602; F=45.432, p=0.000).

Figure 13. Regression Analysis Results in Projectized Organizations – Project Mission and Project Performance

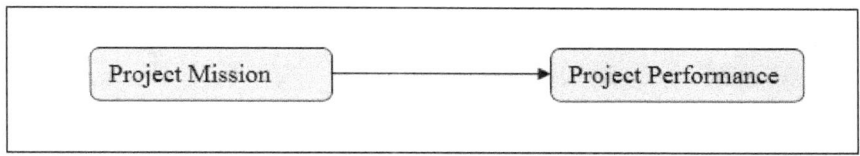

Summary of Hypothesis Testing

Hypothesis	Test Result
A clear project mission has a positive influence on project success and explains the variance in it.	**Accepted**
High support from the top management has a positive influence on project success and explains the variance in it.	Failed to Accept
A detailed project schedule/plan has a positive influence on project success and explains the variance in it.	Failed to Accept
Frequent and high client consultation has a positive influence on project success and explains the variance in it.	**Accepted**
Competent project personnel have a positive influence on project success and explain the variance in it.	Failed to Accept
The availability of technical tasks force has a positive influence on project success and explains the variance in it.	**Accepted**
High client acceptance has a positive influence on project success and explains the variance in it.	Failed to Accept
Frequent monitoring and feedback activity has a positive influence on project success and explains the variance in it.	Failed to Accept
Effective and sufficient communication has a positive influence on project success and explains the variance in it.	Failed to Accept
Capability in trouble-shooting has a positive influence on project success and explains the variance in it.	Failed to Accept
Project duration will moderate the relationship between project mission and project performance.	**Accepted**
Organization structure has a moderating effect on the relationship between monitoring & feedback and project success.	**Accepted**

Table 5. Summary of Hypothesis Testing

11 CONCLUSION

The main focus of the study was to analyze the success criteria in order to identify the project success perception and to analyze the relationship between information technology project performance and critical success factors information technology sector.

11.1. Conclusion of Success Criteria

There is no general agreement or standard on project success definitions or how to measure it (Culleri, 2009; Pinto & Slevin, 1986). Also, in the literature there are no consistent research results related to relationships between project success factors and IT project performance (Culler, 2009; Westlund, 2007; Agirre Perez, 2007; Wu, 2006Hass, 2006; Nasr, 2004).

In this research, the data was collected from IT professionals by an online survey. The sectors of the participants were various like finance/banking, software industry, telecommunications, service & engineering and other sectors as healthcare and government. Although, the questionnaire was long with 73 questions, the number of respondents was quite high – between 326 and 236 - when compared to previous similar researches.

When we looked at the project success criteria it was found that although, project teams generally found their projects as "successful" - 77% - related to their subjective perceptions; only 42% of the projects met their budget targets, 53% had good initial quality and 54% finished their projects in targeted schedules. The results showed that in IT industry, budget, schedule and quality criteria (the iron triangle) had the lowest success percentages between twelve project success criteria.

The highest success ratio in the iron triangle belonged to schedule and the worst ratio belonged to budget. It is normal since being on schedule and deploying new products to market before competitors in order to gain market advantage is generally more important in IT industry – as in other industries - than being in project budget. Despite, these success ratios in the study about budget, quality and schedule were seemed low; the results were parallel to world average. According to PMI's 2012 Pulse of the Profession Benefits Realization In-Depth Report, only about half of software projects meet their original budget and schedule targets.

When we looked at the other criteria, it was found that project team satisfaction in information technology sector was not too high with only 56%. This may be the result of hard work in software development sector related to tight schedules but complicated products. On the other hand, 64% of the project teams believed that they developed the best solutions, despite serious deadlines.

The percentage of the attendees, who believed that their projects would lead to improved decision making of the users was 59%. Where the percentage of the attendees who believed their projects would lead improvement in performance of their users was 69%. Generally projects that aim operational improvements, higher efficiency and automation are higher than decision making effectiveness projects, in IT sector.

Most of the participants believed that their project would have a positive effect for those who made use of it with 74%; also 75% said that intended users benefited the product, 78% said that output of their products worked as planned and 79% believed that project sponsors and important clients made use of the project. Finally, with the highest ratio, participants believed that 83% of the output/products of the projects were used.

As a result, the average project success ratio of twelve success criteria (budget target, quality target, schedule target, team satisfaction, benefit of the users in terms of decision making, best solution, benefit of the users in terms of operational efficiency, positive effect, product benefit, product worked, important client benefit and usage rate of the end product) was 66%.

We saw that although, project development processes was not very successful where budget target, quality target, schedule target and team satisfaction success ratios were low; ratios related to end products and effects of the projects were quite high. On the other hand, this average ratio was still under subjective success perception of team members, 77%, showing that project teams saw their projects as more successful than the projects really were.

11.2. Conclusion of Success Factors

When we looked at the relationship between ten critical project success factors (project mission, top management support, project schedule/planning, client consultation, project team, technical tasks, client acceptance, monitoring and feedback, communication and trouble-shooting) in PIP and project performance, we found three critical success factors, which were effective: project mission, technical tasks and client consultation.

As a result of the study, we saw that a clear project mission had a positive impact on project performance and the most important factor for project success. As we have discussed, project mission involved establishing goals and clearly defining directions for project stakeholders (Project Management Institute, 2008).

In PIP questionnaire, clear project mission factor was measured by if project team believed that the goals of the project were in line with the general goods of the organization, if the goals of the project were made clear to the team, if they believed the results of the project would benefit the organization, if they were enthusiastic about the success of the project and if the team were aware of the beneficial consequences of the project to the organization. As a result, we saw that to clarify the aim of the project and the team to believe the importance of the project and how it would benefit the organization, were the most important factors in order to increase project performance.

Related to our study, another very important critical success factor to increase project performance was technical tasks. As we have defined, this factor involved activities related to accomplishing technical objectives by ensuring the availability of the necessary technology and procedures (Pinto, 1986; Slevin & Pinto, 1986). In our questionnaire availability of technical tasks were measured by if project team was competent, if the team understood the project, if specific project tasks were well managed, if the technology being used supported the project and if appropriate technology was selected. As a consequence of our study, recruiting the competent project team and giving them the right technological infrastructure were critically important to increase project performance.

Client consultation was the final critical success factor that affected project performance. This factor involved including users in the implementation process, providing client status communications and actively listening to all stakeholders (Pinto, 1986; Slevin & Pinto, 1986).

In PIP questionnaire, the contribution of client consultation factor was measured by, if the clients were given opportunity to provide input early in the project development stage, if they were kept informed of the project's progress, if the value and limitations of the project had been discussed with the clients and if the clients were told how their input was considered by the project team. Although our subject was about information technology projects, with this factor we understood the importance of right communication with business clients / end-users and taking their opinions were also critical for IT and technical project performance improvement.

Project duration is the time frame between project initiation and closure phases. Related to 264 answers coming from participants, the average information technology project duration was 9 months. As hypothesized, it was found that project duration moderated the relationship between critical success factors and project performance. Related to our study, project duration negatively affected project performance, as project duration increased project performance decreased.

Moreover, one of the purposes of the study was to determine if organization structure moderated the effect on the relationship between critical success factors and project performance. As a result of our analysis, we found out that troubleshooting critical success factor had positive contribution on project performance in functional organizations. For weak matrix organizations, only technical tasks had a positive contribution on project performance. Also, we found out that both project mission and technical tasks critical success factors had positive contribution on project performance in strong matrix organizations. Finally, for projectized organizations project mission critical success factor was the only factor that affected project performance. As a result of these findings, we said that organization structure type had a moderating effect on the relationship between success factors and project performance.

12 IMPLICATIONS FOR MANAGEMENT

During the last decades, we witnessed the born of personal computers, internet, workflow softwares, mobile devices and services. Today, it is possible for more people than ever to compete and collaborate in real time from different corners of the world and on an equal basis than at any other previous time in the history of the world by using fiber-optic networks, computers, e-mail and teleconferencing (Friedman, 2005).

Information technology also allows organizations to improve operational efficiency and control, as well as compete in a rapidly changing environment. Corporations are increasingly using IT strategies to provide business units with competitive advantage, spending $2 trillion annually worldwide on information technology (Wheelen & Hunger, 2010). As a result, today, IT projects have a key role on the implementation and execution of company strategies.

Although investment and importance of IT related projects are growing dramatically, these projects are often behind schedules, over budgeted and not meeting stakeholder expectations. This study presents managers, what is understood from project performance and which factors are important for more successful projects.

The project success criteria findings of our study show that especially the success criteria related with project planning targets (budget, quality, and schedule) are quite low.

One reason of this problem may be the lack of time needed for detailed project planning. For a detailed planning, IT project teams responsible from forecasting and planning should come together with each other and with the business people in order to understand their needs and determine the necessary technical solutions, allocate necessary human and technological resources.

Typically, this process takes weeks for the necessity of organizing meetings with various stakeholders and trying to make decisions. On the business side some projects may have more than one sponsor and owner, on the IT side project teams may be formed from different divisions with tens of IT professionals. As a result, if managements do not support and do not spare necessary time to project teams for planning, they should know that most probably they will miss their project schedule, budget and quality targets.

Moreover most of the time business people force IT people to shorten or compress their forecasted targets, related to strategic objectives. As a result of this time pressure from management, usually IT teams have to undersign project targets that they don't think as achievable. These kinds of interventions also decrease the motivation and morale of the project teams, which is also observed as low team satisfaction in our research. As a consequence, IT managements should listen to their project teams and resist to these kinds of business pressures for unachievable targets.

Another typical reason is the change requests that come out after project planning phase. Since typical IT projects last for a couple of months and sometimes exceed a year, it is natural for today's fast changing world for business stakeholders to change their requests; no matter how detailed they had thought during the project planning phase. On the other hand, each change about a project affects the initial project scope on which the planning was done. When the project scope changes, it should not be expected to keep the initial budget, quality and schedule targets. Since there may be more than one business sponsors, owners and stakeholders, lots of different change requests may come from different parties for the same project.

Here, with the coordination of the project manager, project sponsors and business managers should decide which change requests are crucial and which are not. Only necessary change requests should be taken into consideration and new project baselines should be taken for new project targets. At this point, the importance of change management takes place. PMBOK defines integrated change control as "the process of reviewing all change requests; approving changes and managing changes to deliverables, organizational process assets, project documents, and the project management plan; and communicating their disposition." It reviews all requests for changes or modifications to project documents, deliverables, baselines, or the project management plan and approves or rejects the changes.

The key benefit of this process is that it allows for documented changes within the project to be considered in an integrated fashion while reducing project risk, which often arises from changes made without consideration to the overall project objectives or plans. Therefore, IT managements should be sure that project change management processes are working properly in their organizations.

In summary, in order to improve project success criteria findings, especially project execution targets, managers should give special importance to project planning phase and change control process.

On the critical success factors side, we found three factors that affect project success: project mission, technical tasks and client consultation. Managements should concentrate on these factors to meet their target project schedules, budgets, qualities, team satisfactions and for project outputs that lead to customer satisfaction and customer welfare in terms of decision making and performance improvements.

As we have found out, project mission is the most important factor for a successful project. Therefore, organizations should be sure that the aim of their IT projects are well understood by the project teams, these teams should believe the positive consequences of these studies and should be enthusiastic about the success of these projects. On the other hand, especially in large organizations, business people who request the projects and IT teams who develop them are located in different organizational divisions, with different priorities.

As an example, a marketing team who requests a very different credit card concentrates on the market share and profit that will gain with the new product when it launches. But, the IT team who will develop the credit card concentrates on the technical details. Although, the new product is very important and maybe strategic for the organization, it may be just another ordinary development project for the IT team. As a result, necessary actions should be taken in order to bring together different parties and motivate them to work for the same objective.

For example, during initiation phase, business teams and IT teams should come together as much as necessary, in order IT teams to understand, what is requested by the business, why this project is important for the organization and what strategic objectives will be fulfilled by completing the project.

As well as, business side should understand what their technical alternatives are, what the technical limitations are and how their requests will be fulfilled by the IT team. In the planning phase, business side should communicate when they will need which feature and why they need it. Correspondingly, IT team should explain when they will deliver which future and why.

Most of the time, business needs and technical necessities do not match at the requested time as a result of scarcity of human and technical resources. At this point, stakeholders should come together as much as possible in order to understand each other and agree on the best plan. When IT teams understand and believe the importance and the aim of the project request, they will present optimum solutions for the optimum times, which is crucial for a successful project.

The second most important factor for successful IT projects is the technical tasks. In today's world, it is quite easy to reach necessary software and technology from any party of the world. The determining technical factor which differentiates successful projects from unsuccessful ones is the human resources. For example, most successful web sites like Amazon, eBay or LinkedIn have the same technological infrastructure as other millions of web sites. Although the infrastructures are the same, the successful ones are differentiated from ordinary ones as a result of different contents, designs and services that are imagined and developed by the project teams. The situation is the same in any other ordinary IT project. Beginning from the initiation to closure phases, human resources is the determining factor in IT projects.

If you have competent technical people in your team, you can understand the project mission better, you can plan it in a more detailed way, foresee the risks and manage them more easily, as a result you face less problems in the execution phase and you can close the project more easily. It is management's responsibility to recruit the competent project team, to train them if necessary, allocate them to related tasks on time and give them the right technological infrastructure, in order to increase project performance.

The third and the last critical factor for successful projects is the client consultation. Every project is a cost until it is deployed for customer use. The organization starts the get profit for its investment not during the project but, after it is used by the intended users and customers.

IT project teams should work close to business stakeholders, who will use the output of the project. If business owners do not own these outputs and not use the products, the projects will be only costs to the related organizations without benefits.

In order to achieve customer input, project teams should be open to communication with their clients by beginning the project with a formal kick-off, issuing project status reports periodically, arranging status and phase meetings periodically, taking necessary approvals when business analysis is finished, planning user acceptance tests in order clients to test the output before it goes live, taking necessary client approvals before project deployment and arranging project closure meetings before closing the project. As a result, IT managements should establish the necessary processes as described above to be sure to take client input in projects in order to be successful.

Another important finding of our research is that as the project duration increases the project performance decreases. Typically in practice, we observe decrease in focus of project teams and business stakeholders as duration of projects increase. Also, for long duration projects, the aim of the projects may change and new needs may come up, stakeholders may confuse about the main objectives of the project as time passes, people working on the projects may change, other urgent projects and tasks may come up. In order to prevent from this negative effect, IT professionals and managers should aim their project plans to be as short as possible.

If it is not possible due to complexity of project scope, project team should aim iterative planning by delivering incremental components of business functionality in shorter durations. For example, instead of planning a one year project, project team may plan three iterations or phases, where they will deliver the first output in three months, a second output in six months and the final one at the end of the project. As a result, all stakeholders may focus to the first deliverable at the beginning of the project, than they will focus on the second deliverable at the middle of their studies and finally focus on the final deliverables at the end of the project. By this way, project stakeholders may not lose their concentrations as a result of distant targets.

Also, most of the professionals work for more than one project at the same time which decreases focus. Instead of finishing a current project and starting another, companies choose to start projects in parallel with same teams, which result generally project duration extension.

As a result, instead of parallel functioning, efficiency of teams can be increased by ensuring them to work on only one project during specific project time, as much as possible.

Finally, when we look at the organizational structure organizational structure effect, we clearly see that this variable moderates the relationship between critical success factors and project performance. Related to our research, troubleshooting critical success factor had positive contribution on project performance in functional organizations. This means if you are handling problems successfully when they arise, your project performance will increase in functional organizations. When we look at our research questionnaire, we see that the questions related to this factor are generally about foreseeing problems before they arise, knowing what to do and getting necessary support – even from people out of project team - as quick as possible when problems arise. In functional organizations, since project managers don't have much authority and functional tasks are more important than project tasks, it is hard for project manager / leader or the project team to focus on projects and take necessary actions quickly due to functional barriers and priorities. Related to these barriers and difficulties, functional organizations are the least preferred types (8%) as mentioned in our study. We see that for other types of organizations, technical tasks and project mission success factors were the most important for high project performance.

In weak matrix organizations technical tasks are the most important factor. As we have mentioned before, this factor involved recruiting the competent project team and giving them the right technological infrastructure. Since, in weak matrix organizations project managers' role involves only coordination, we can hardly talk about a team. As a result, establishment of a competent team, giving them the right technological infrastructure and managing their tasks gain importance.

However, in projectized organizations, since competent project teams are formed for specific projects and project managers have the necessary authority, project mission aroused as the most important success factor. This shows us that, when these teams understand the aim, details of the project and believe the project, they get more successful. For strong matrix organizations, which are a mixture of weak matrix and projectized organizations, both project mission and technical tasks were important.

As a result of our study, we can say that by preferring projectized organizations, IT managers may avoid problems arousing from incompetent project teams or incompetent project management, and concentrate on project teams' understanding project mission and motivation.

Finally, our findings generally point out agile project management frameworks, where single focused (projectized organization) dedicated (project mission) cross-functional teams (technical tasks) are formed who work close to business product owners (client consultation) and act in an iterative – incremental way to deploy project deliverables in the shortest possible time (project duration).

chapter ten text here. Insert chapter ten text here.

REFERENCES

Agirre Perez, I. (2007). Stochastic project scheduling system: Implications for risk management. Dissertation Abstracts International, 68 (2). (UMI No.3252325)

Alfi, S. J., (2002). A study of the relationship between project managers' tenure, education, training, experience, and project manager success. A dissertation presented to the Faculty of the Graduate School of Education and Psychology Pepperdine University.

Anonymous. (July 2012). The power of benefits realization. PMI Network, 26 (7), 16-17.

Anonymous. (June 2013). Strong but vulnerable. The Economist Newspaper Limited; available from http://www.economist.com/news/europe/21579491-turkey-remains-highly-exposed-loss-confidence-foreign-investors-strong-vulnerable; Internet; accessed 27 April 2014.

Anonymous. (Jan 2014). The mask is off. The Economist Newspaper Limited; avaible from http://www.economist.com/news/finance-and-economics/21593496-political-turmoil-exposes-economic-malaise-mask; Internet; accessed 27 April 2014.

Anonymous. (April 2014). Definition of project success. Chaos Activity News 9(4; available from http://www.standishgroup.com/chaos_news/newsletter.php?id=70; Internet; accessed 06 May 2014.

Anonymous, (2014). Project. Merriam-Webster Incorporated, available from http://www.merriam-webster.com/dictionary/project, Internet; accessed 18 May 2014.

APM (2006). APM body of knowledge. 5th Edition. High Wycombe, UK: The Association for Project Management.

Avots, I., 1969. Why does project management fail? California Management Review, 12, 77–82.

Baker, B.N., Murphy,D.C., & Fischer,D. (1974). Factors affecting project success. In D.I. Cleland & W.R. King (Eds), Project

Management Handbook (pp. 902-919). New York: Van Nostrand Reinhold.

Baccarni, D. (1999). The logical framework method for defining project success. Project Management Journal, 30(4), 25-32.

Belassi, W. and Tukel, O.I., 1996. A new framework for determining critical success/failure factors in projects. International Journal of Project Management, 14 (3), 141–151.

Belout, A. and Gauvreau, C., 2004. Factors influencing project success: the impact of HRM. International Journal of Project Management, 22 (1), 1–11.

Cicmil, S. & Hodgson, D. (2006). New possibilities for project management theory: A critical engagement. Project Management Journal, 37(3), 111-122.

Cleland, D.I. (1999). Project Management: Strategic Design and Implementation (3rd ed.). New York: McGraw-Hill.

Cooke-Davies, T., 2002. The real success factors on project. International Journal of Project Management, 20 (3), 185–190.

Crawford, J. K. & Pennypacker, J. S. (2002, October). Put an End to Project Mismanagement. 73-78.

Creswell, J. W. (2005). Educational Research: Planning, Conducting, and Evaluating Quantitative and Qualitative Research (2nd ed.). Upper Saddle River, NJ: Prentice-Hall.

Culler, E.W. (2009). The Degree of Relationship Between Critical Success Factors and Information Technology Project Performance. University of Phoenix. (UMI No. 3381832)

Declerck, R., Debourse, J., & Declerck, J. (1997). Le management stratégique: contrôle de l'irréversibilité. Lille: Les éditions ESC Lille.

Declerck, R., Debourse, J. & Navarre, C. (1983). La Méthode de Direction générale : le management stratégique. Paris: Hommes et Techniques.

Delisle, C. L. G. (2001). Success and communication in virtual project teams.

Dissertation Abstracts International, 62 (12), 4242. (UMI No. NQ64855)

DeVellis, R. F. (2003). Scale development: Theory and applications (2nd ed.). London:Sage.

Dogan, F. (February 2014). 6 markets to watch. PMI Network, 28 (2), 33.

Durmuş, B., Yurtkoru, E.S., and Çinko, M., 2011. Sosyal Bilimlerde SPSS'le Veri Analizi (4ncü Baskı).

Dvir, D., Lipovetsky, S., Shenhar, A., and Tishler, A., 1998. In search of project classification: a nonuniversal approach to project success factors. Research policy, 27, 915–935.

Ewusi-Mensah, K. (1997). Critical issues in abandoned information systems development projects: What is it about IS projects that make susceptible to cancellations? Communications of the ACM, 40(9), 74-80.

Finch, P. (2003). Applying the Slevin-Pinto Project Implementation Profile to an
information systems project. Project Management Journal, 34(3), 32-39.

Frame, J. D. (2003). Managing projects in organizations: How to make the best use of time, techniques, and people (3rd ed.). San Francisco: Jossey-Bass.

Friedman, T.L. (2005). The World Is Flat: A Brief History of the 21st Century (1st Edition), New York: Farrar, Straus and Giroux.

Glen, P. (2005). The truth about 'useless' people. Computerworld, 39(27), 34. Retrieved May 15, 2008, Academic Search Alumni Edition database.

Hair, J.F., et al., (2006). Multivariate Data Analysis (6th edition), New York: Macmillion Publishing Company.

Hartman, F. & Ashrafi, R.I. (2002). Project management in the information systems and IT industries. Project Management Journal, 33(3), 5-15.

Hass, K. (2006). The five deadly sins of project management. Power, 150(9), 82-85.

Hawk, D., 2006. Conditions of success: a platform for international construction development. Construction management and economies, 24 (7), 735–742.

Hazebroucq, J.-M. (1993). Les facteurs cles de succes dans le management de projets. Revue Inyernationale en Management et Gestion de Projets, 1(1), 27-40.

Heerkens, G. R. (2002). Project management (The briefcase book). New York, NY: McGraw-Hill.

Hughes, M.W., 1986. Why projects fail: the effects of ignoring the obvious. Industrial engineering, 18, 14–18.

Hyvari, I., 2005. Project management effectiveness in project-oriented business organizations. International journal of project management, 23, 101–112.

Hyväri, I. (2006). Success of projects in different organizational conditions. Project Management Journal, 37(4), 31-41.

Ika, L.A., 2009. Project success as a topic in project management journals. Project Management Journal 40 (4), 6–19.

International Project Management Association (2006), ICB – IPMA competence baseline, version 3.0. International Project Management Association. Zurich, Switzerland.

International Project Management Institution. (2014). IPMA History. International Project Management Institution; available from http://ipma.ch/about/ipma-history/; Internet; accessed 20 April 2014.

Istanbul Project Management Association (IPYD). (2014). IPYD About Us, Istanbul Project Management Association, available from http://www.ipyd.org/CategoryDetail.aspx?ID=3; Internet; accessed 23 April 2014.

Jones, B. (2007). Factors affecting the full and successful implementation of new technology supporting national security: Analysis of the implementation of the Single Mobility System. Dissertation Abstracts International, 68 (09). (UMI No. 3277630)

Jugdev, K., & Müller, R. (2005). A retrospective look at our evolving understanding of project success. Project Management Journal, 36(4), 19-31.

Karlsen, J., et al., 2006. An empirical study of critical success factors in IT projects. International Journal of Management and Enterprise Development, 3 (4), 292–311.

Karayaz, G. & Gungor, O. (2013). Strategic alignment and project management offices: case studies from successful implementations in Turkey. 46th Hawaii International Conference on System Sciences, 4374-4383.

Kerzner, H. (2006). Project management, a systems approach to planning, scheduling, and controlling. (9th ed.). Hoboken, NJ: John-Wiley & Sons.

Kerzner, H. (2010). Project management best practices. (2nd ed.). Hoboken, NJ: John-Wiley & Sons.

Koca, F. (2014). Pmbok and Prince2: Really comparable? PMI Turkey Chapter E-Bulletin 2-1, available from http://www.gokremtekir.com/wp-content/uploads/2014/04/PMI_TR_e-Buten_Mart2014.pdf; Internet; accessed 23 April 2014.

Kuen C.W., Zailani S., & Fernando Y. (2009). Critical factors influencing the project success amongst manufacturing companies in Malaysia. African Journal of Business Management, 3 (1), 16-27.

Lang, R. D. (2007). Project leadership: Key elements and critical success factors for IT project managers. Journal of Healthcare Information Management, 21(1), 2-4.

Leedy, P., & Ormrod, J. (2005). Practical research: Planning and design (8th ed.). Upper Saddle River, NJ: Prentice Hall.

Likert, R. (1932). A technique for the measurement of attitudes [Abstract]. Archives of Psychology, 22(140), 5-53.

Lim, C.S., & Mohamed, M.Z. (1999). Criteria of project success: An explanatory re-examination. International Journal of Project Management, 17, 243-248.

Lock, D. (2003). Project Management, Gower Publishing, Eighth edition.

Mahaney, R.C. & Lederer, A.L. (2006). The effect of intrinsic and extrinsic rewards for developers on information systems project success. Project Management Journal, 37(4), 42-54.

Marchewka, J.T. (2006). Information technology project management: Providing measurable organizational value (2nd ed.). Hoboken, NJ: John Wiley and Sons.

Meredith J.R., Raturi A., Amaoako-Gyampah K. & Kaplan B. (1989). Alternative Research Paradigms in Operations. Journal of Operations Management, 8(4), 297-326.

Morris, P.W. and Hough, G.H., 1987. The anatomy of major projects. New York: JohnWiley and Son.

Munns, A.K., & Bjeirmi, B.F. (1996). The role of project management in achieving project success. International Journal of Project Management, 14, 81-87.

Murch, R. (2001). Project management: Best practices for IT professionals (1st ed.). Saddle River, NJ: Prentice Hall.

Murphy, D., Baker, N. and Fisher, D. (1974). Determinants of Project Success, Boston College, National Aeronautics and Space Administration, Boston.

Nasr, E. B. (2004). An integrated project planning and control system approach for measuring project performance. Dissertation Abstracts International, 66 (03), 1608B. (UMI No. 3168289)

Neuman, W. L. (2003). Social research methods: Qualitative and quantitative approaches (5th ed.). Boston: Allyn & Bacon.

OGC (2007). Managing successful programmes (3rd edition). Norwich, UK: Office of Government Commerce.

Oren, R.A. (2009). Contributory success factors for projects with the project management profession: A quantitative analysis. (UMI No. 3368756)

Pinto, J. K. (1986). Project implementation: A determination of its critical success factors, moderators, and their relative importance across the project life cycle. Dissertation Abstracts International, 48 (04), 981A. (UMI No. 8707585)

Pinto, J. K., & Prescott, J. E. (1988). Variations in critical success factors over the stages in the project life cycle. Journal of Management 14, 5-18. Retrieved August 9, 2008, from Business Source Complete database.

Pinto, J. K., & Slevin, D. P. (1988). Project Success: Definitions and Measurement Techniques. Project Management Journal, 19(1), 67–72.

Pinto, J. K., & Slevin, D. P. (1989). Critical success factors in R&D projects. Research Technology Management, 32, 31. Retrieved February 24, 2008, from ABI/INFORM Global database.

Proabhakar, G.P. (2008). Projects and their management: A literature review. International Journal of Business and Management, August 2008, 3-9.

Projects in Controlled Environments. (2014). Home. PRINCE2; available from http://www.prince-officialsite.com/; Internet accessed 21 April 2014.

Project Management Institute. (2008). A guide to the project management body of knowledge (PMBOK guide) (4th ed.). Newtown Square, PA: Author.

Project Management Institute. (2013). 2012 Annual Report: Enhancing business value around the world. Project Management Institute; available from http://www.pmi.org/About-Us/~/media/PDF/Publications/PMI%202012%20Annual%20Repor t.ashx; Internet; accessed 20 April 2014.

Project Management Institute (2013). A guide to the project management body of knowledge (PMBOK guide) (5th ed.). Newtown Square, PA: Author.

Project Management Institute. (2014). About Us. Project Management Institute; available from http://www.pmi.org/About-Us.aspx; Internet; accessed 20 April 2014.

Project Management Institute Turkey Chapter. (2014). News Letter. Project

Management Institute Turkey; available from http://www.pmi.org.tr/c7/tr/haber-buelteni.html; Internet; accessed 23 April 2014.

Republic of Turkey Ministry of Development. (2014). About Us. Republic of Turkey Ministry of Development; available from http://www.mod.gov.tr/Pages/Overview.aspx; Internet; accessed 27 April 2014.

Richman, L. (2002). Successful project management (2nd ed.). New York: AMACOM, a division of American Management Association International.

Robbins, S.P. and Judge, T.A. (2009) Organizational behavior (13th ed.). New Jersey, Pearson Education Incorporation.

Rubin, I.M. and Seeling, W., 1967. Experience as a factor in the selection and performance of project managers. IEEE transactions of engineering management, 14 (3), 131–134.

Sarı, A. (2011). PMI Turkey chapter is growing. PMI Turkey, available from http://pmday2011.pmi.bg/Content/Asli%20Sari/2011%2010-11%20PMI%20Bulgaria%20v4-%206%2011%202011.pdf; Internet; accessed 20 April 2014.

Sekaran, U. (2003). Research methods for business (4th ed.). USA: John Wiley & Sons.

Seymour, D.E., Hoare, D.J., & Itau, L. (1992). Project Management Leadership Styles: Problems of resolving the continuity-change dilemma, 11th INTERNET World Congress on Project Management, Florence: Italy.

Scrum Alliance. (2014). About Us. Scrum Alliance; available from http://www.scrumalliance.org/about-us; Internet; accessed 23 April 2014.

Shenhar, A. J., Dvir, D., Milosevic, D., Mulenburg, J., Patanakul, P., Reilly, et al. (2005). Toward a NASA-specific project management framework. Engineering Management Journal, 17(4), 8-14.

Shenhar, A. J., & Dvir, D. (2007). Project management research – The challenge and opportunity. Project Management Journal, 38(2), 93-99.

Slevin, D. P., & Pinto, J. K. (1986). The project implementation profile:

New tool for project managers [Abstract]. Project Management Journal, 17(4), 57-71.

Slevin, D. P., & Pinto, J. K. (1987). Balancing strategy and tactics in project implementation. Sloan Management Review, 29, 33-41. Retrieved February 24, 2008, from ABI/INFORM Global database.

Standish Group. (2003). Latest Standish Group CHAOS report shows project success rates have improved by 50%. Retrieved July 7, 2007, from http://www.standishgroup.com/press/article.php?id=2

The World Bank Group. (2014). GDP Ranking. The World Bank Group; available from http://data.worldbank.org/data-catalog/GDP-ranking-table; Internet; accessed 27 April 2014.

Thiry, M. (2010). Program management. Gower Publishing Company. Farnham, UK.

Tuman, G.J. (1983). Development and implementation of effective project management information and control systems, in Cleland, D.I. & King, W.R. (eds.) Project management handbook. New York: Van Nostrand Reinhold Co., 495-532.

Turner, J.R. (1999) The handbook of project-based management: improving the processes for achieving strategic objectives. 2nd ed. London: McGraw-Hill

Wateridge, J. (1998). How can IS/IT projects be measured for success? International Journal of Project Management, 16, 59-63.

Weber, M. (1964). The theory of social and economic organization. New York: The Free Press of Glencoe.

Westlund, S. G. (2007). Retaining talent: Assessing relationships among project leadership styles, software developer job satisfaction, and turnover intentions. Dissertation Abstracts International, 68 (11). (UMI No. 3288701)

Wheelen, T.L. and Hunger, J.D. (2010). Strategic Management and Business Policy (12th Edition). New Jersey: Pearson Education.

Wu, W. W. (2006). IT personnel sourcing decisions in IT projects. Dissertation Abstracts International, 67 (1). (UMI No. 3206973)

APPENDIX

Project Success Perception & Critical Success Factors Affecting Project Performance Survey

Demographic Information

Gender (X):   Female ☐   Male ☐

Age: _____

Education Degree: High School / Undergraduate / Graduate / PhD

Job Experience (X):

☐ Less than 1 year   ☐ 1 – 5 years   ☐ 6 – 10 years

☐ 11 – 15 years   ☐ 16 – 20 years   ☐ More than 20 years

Project Role (X):

☐ Project Team Member   ☐ Resource Manager/Leader   ☐ Project
☐ Manager/Leader   ☐ Project Sponsor

Sector Information (X):

☐ Finance / Banking   ☐ Telecommunications ☐ Software

☐ Engineering   ☐ Service   ☐ Health

☐ Government   ☐ Others

Project Information

Project Team Size:

☐ Up to 10   ☐ 11 – 20   ☐ 21 - 30   ☐ 31 – 40

☐ 41 – 50   ☐ 51 – 100   ☐ More than 100

Project Duration (Months): _____

Organization Structure (X):

☐ Functional Organization: Resource managers / team leaders are responsible from project decisions / results. There are no other project managers / leaders.

☐ Weak Matrix: Resource managers / team leaders are the main responsible from project decisions / results. Project managers / leaders do coordination and reporting.

☐ Strong Matrix: Both resource managers / team leaders and project managers / leaders are equally responsible from project decisions / results.

☐ Project Based Organization: Project managers / leaders are responsible from project decisions / results. There are no other resource managers / team leaders.

PIP – Project Performance Criteria

Instructions

Questions should be answered by choosing one of the alternatives provided, and there are no "correct" or "incorrect" answers.

The questions relate to your evaluation of the ultimate performance of the project in which you were involved. Please indicate the appropriate number the extent to which you agree or disagree with the following statements as they relate to outcome of the project.

		Strongly Disagree	Disagree	Somewhat Disagree	Neutral	Somewhat Agree	Agree	Strongly Agree
1	This project has come in on schedule.	1	2	3	4	5	6	7
2	This project has come in on budget	1	2	3	4	5	6	7
3	The project that has been developed works.	1	2	3	4	5	6	7
4	The project will be/is used by its intended clients.	1	2	3	4	5	6	7
5	This project has/will directly benefit the intended users: either through increasing efficiency or employee effectiveness.	1	2	3	4	5	6	7
6	Given the problem for which it was developed, this project seems to do the best job of solving the problem, i.e., it was the best choice among the set of alternatives.	1	2	3	4	5	6	7
7	Important clients, directly affected by this project, will make use of it.	1	2	3	4	5	6	7
8	I am/was satisfied with the process by which this project is being/was completed.	1	2	3	4	5	6	7
9	We are confident that non-technical start-up problems will be minimal, because the project will be readily accepted by its intended users.	1	2	3	4	5	6	7
10	Use of this project has/will directly lead to improve or more effective decision making or performance for the clients	1	2	3	4	5	6	7
11	This project will have a positive impact on those who make use of it.	1	2	3	4	5	6	7
12	The results of this project represent a definite improvement in performance over the way clients used to perform these activities.	1	2	3	4	5	6	7
13	All things considered, this project was a success.	1	2	3	4	5	6	7

PIP - Factor Contributions

Instructions

Questions should be answered by choosing one of the alternatives provided, and there are no "correct" or "incorrect" answers.

This part of the questionnaire attempts to measure the relative contribution of the following 10 factors to the project's final outcome and subsequent performance. Please indicate the appropriate number the extent to which you agree or disagree with the following statements as they relate to activities occurring in the project about which you are reporting.

A.	Project Mission	Strongly Disagree	Disagree	Somewhat Disagree	Neutral	Somewhat Agree	Agree	Strongly Agree
1	The goals of the project are in line with the general goals of the organization.	1	2	3	4	5	6	7
2	The basic goals of the project are made clear to the project team.	1	2	3	4	5	6	7
3	The results of the project will benefit the parent organization.	1	2	3	4	5	6	7
4	I am enthusiastic about the chances for success of this project.	1	2	3	4	5	6	7
5	I am aware of and can identify the beneficial consequences to the organization of success of this project.	1	2	3	4	5	6	7

B.	Management Support	Strongly Disagree	Disagree	Somewhat Disagree	Neutral	Somewhat Agree	Agree	Strongly Agree
1	Upper management is responsive to our requests for additional resources, if the need arises.	1	2	3	4	5	6	7
2	Upper management shares responsibility with the project team for ensuring the project's success.	1	2	3	4	5	6	7
3	I agree with upper management on the degree of my authority and responsibility for the project.	1	2	3	4	5	6	7
4	Upper management will support me in a crisis.	1	2	3	4	5	6	7
5	Upper management has granted us the necessary authority and will support our decisions concerning the project.	1	2	3	4	5	6	7

C.	Project Schedule/Plan	Strongly Disagree	Disagree	Somewhat Disagree	Neutral	Somewhat Agree	Agree	Strongly Agree
1	We know which activities contain slack time or slack resources which can be utilized in other areas during emergencies.	1	2	3	4	5	6	7
2	There is a detailed plan (including time schedules, milestones, and manpower requirements) for the completion of the project.	1	2	3	4	5	6	7
3	There is a detailed budget for the project.	1	2	3	4	5	6	7
4	Key personnel needs (who, when) are specified in the project plan.	1	2	3	4	5	6	7
5	There are contingency plans in case the project is off schedule or off budget.	1	2	3	4	5	6	7

D.	Client Consultation	Strongly Disagree	Disagree	Somewhat Disagree	Neutral	Somewhat Agree	Agree	Strongly Agree
1	The clients were given the opportunity to provide input early in the project development stage.	1	2	3	4	5	6	7
2	The clients (intended users) are kept informed of the project's progress.	1	2	3	4	5	6	7
3	The value of the project has been discussed with the eventual clients.	1	2	3	4	5	6	7
4	The limitations of the project have been discussed with the clients (what the project is not designed to do).	1	2	3	4	5	6	7
5	The clients were told whether or not their input was assimilated into the project plan.	1	2	3	4	5	6	7

E.	Project Team	Strongly Disagree	Disagree	Somewhat Disagree	Neutral	Somewhat Agree	Agree	Strongly Agree
1	Project team personnel understand their role on the project team.	1	2	3	4	5	6	7
2	There is sufficient manpower to complete the project.	1	2	3	4	5	6	7
3	The personnel on the project team understand how their performance will be evaluated.	1	2	3	4	5	6	7
4	Job descriptions for team members have been written and distributed and are understood.	1	2	3	4	5	6	7
5	Adequate technical and/or managerial training (and time for training) is available for members of the project team.	1	2	3	4	5	6	7

F.	Technical Tasks	Strongly Disagree	Disagree	Somewhat Disagree	Neutral	Somewhat Agree	Agree	Strongly Agree
1	Specific project tasks are well managed.	1	2	3	4	5	6	7
2	The project engineers and other technical people are competent.	1	2	3	4	5	6	7
3	The technology that is being used to support the project works well.	1	2	3	4	5	6	7
4	The appropriate technology (equipment, training programs, etc.) has been selected for the project success.	1	2	3	4	5	6	7
5	The people implementing this project understand it.	1	2	3	4	5	6	7

G.	Client Acceptance	Strongly Disagree	Disagree	Somewhat Disagree	Neutral	Somewhat Agree	Agree	Strongly Agree
1	There is adequate documentation of the project to permit easy use by the clients (instructions, etc.).	1	2	3	4	5	6	7
2	Potential clients have been contacted about the usefulness of the project.	1	2	3	4	5	6	7
3	An adequate presentation of the project has been developed for the clients.	1	2	3	4	5	6	7
4	Clients know how to contact when problems or questions arise.	1	2	3	4	5	6	7
5	Adequate advanced preparation has been done to determine how best to "sell" the project to clients.	1	2	3	4	5	6	7

H.	Monitoring and Feedback	Strongly Disagree	Disagree	Somewhat Disagree	Neutral	Somewhat Agree	Agree	Strongly Agree
1	All important aspects of the project are monitored, including measures that will provide a complete picture of the project's progress (adherence to budget and schedule, manpower and equipment utilization, team morale, etc.).	1	2	3	4	5	6	7
2	Regular meetings to monitor project progress and improve the feedback to the project team are conducted.	1	2	3	4	5	6	7
3	Actual progress is regularly compared with the project schedule.	1	2	3	4	5	6	7
4	The results of the project reviews are regularly shared with all projects personnel who have impact upon budget and schedule.	1	2	3	4	5	6	7
5	When the budget or schedule requires revision, input is solicited from the project team.	1	2	3	4	5	6	7

I.	Communication	Strongly Disagree	Disagree	Somewhat Disagree	Neutral	Somewhat Agree	Agree	Strongly Agree
1	The results (decisions made, information received and needed, etc.) of planning meetings are published and distributed to applicable personnel.	1	2	3	4	5	6	7
2	Individuals/groups supplying input have received feedback on the acceptance or rejection of their input.	1	2	3	4	5	6	7
3	When the budget or schedule is revised, the changes and the reasons for the changes are communicated to all members of the project team.	1	2	3	4	5	6	7
4	The reason for the changes to existing policies/procedures have been explained to members of the project team, other groups affected by the changes, and upper management.	1	2	3	4	5	6	7
5	All groups affected by the project know how to make problems known to the project team.	1	2	3	4	5	6	7

J.	Troubleshooting	Strongly Disagree	Disagree	Somewhat Disagree	Neutral	Somewhat Agree	Agree	Strongly Agree
1	The project leader is not hesitant to enlist the aid of personnel not involved in the project in the event of problems.	1	2	3	4	5	6	7
2	"Brain storming" sessions are held to determine where problems are most likely to occur.	1	2	3	4	5	6	7
3	In case of project difficulties, project team members know exactly where to go for assistance.	1	2	3	4	5	6	7
4	I am confident that problems that arise can be solved completely.	1	2	3	4	5	6	7
5	Immediate action is taken when problems come to the project team's attention.	1	2	3	4	5	6	7

ABOUT THE AUTHOR

Dr. Burak Uluocak has more than 18 years of experience in information technology and banking sectors. He took part in large scale projects as Business Analyst, System Analyst, Project Leader, Scrum Master, Project/Program and Portfolio Manager. For the last 3 years, he has been working in a bank as the Vice President of IT Agile Project Management Office and Architecture, responsible from PMO, Agile Studio, System Architecture and Business Process Management Center of Excellence divisions.

Concentrated on management theories and practices, he has engineering, MBA degrees and he is Ph.D. in Strategic Management field. He has Project Management Professional, Certified Scrum Master, Professional Scrum Master and professional coach certifications. He attended many national and international conferences as a speaker about project management and organizational agile transformation subjects.

Burak Uluocak lives in İstanbul with his wife and daughter. He likes sports, latin dances, jazz and of course reading.